The Carmichael Lectures, 1918

LECTURES
ON THE
ANCIENT HISTORY OF INDIA

The Carmichael Lectures, 1918

LECTURES ON THE ANCIENT HISTORY OF INDIA

ON THE PERIOD FROM 650 TO 325 B.C.

Delivered in February, 1918

D. R. BHANDARKAR, M.A., F.A.S.B.,

CARMICHAEL PROFESSOR OF ANCIENT INDIAN HISTORY AND CULTURE, CALCUTTA UNIVERSITY

GYAN

Published by

GYAN

Gyan Publishing House
5, Ansari Road
Daryaganj, New Delhi-110002
Phone: 011-47034999, 9811692060
E-mail: books@gyanbooks.com

Distribution Network
gyanbooks.com
India, USA, Canada, UK, Australia, France

ISBN : 978-81-212-4532-6 (HB)
First Published, 1919

2nd Impression 2020

Printed at: Gyan Press, Delhi.

The Carmichael Lectures, 1918

LECTURES

ON THE

ANCIENT HISTORY OF INDIA

ON THE PERIOD FROM 650 TO 325 B.C.

Delivered in February, 1918

BY

D. R. BHANDARKAR, M.A., F.A.S.B.,

CARMICHAEL PROFESSOR OF ANCIENT INDIAN HISTORY AND CULTURE
CALCUTTA UNIVERSITY

PUBLISHED BY THE

UNIVERSITY OF CALCUTTA

1919

SIR ASUTOSH MOOKERJEE SARASVATI

To

SIR ASUTOSH MOOKERJEE, SARASVATI,

Sastra-Vachaspati, Sambuddhagama-Chakravarti

who, by his lofty ideals,

far-reaching foresight, and unfailing vigilance,

has elevated the Calcutta University to the rank

of a teaching and research University,

the only one of its kind in India,

and who, by his unstinted and discriminate

liberality and encouragement,

has led votaries of learning to look upon him

as the VIKRAMADITYA of the present age,

These Lectures

are dedicated by the Author

in token of profound admiration and reverence.

PREFACE

This book contains the lectures which I delivered as Carmichael Professor of the Calcutta University in February, 1918. When I came here to hold the chair, I was told that I was to deliver four lectures embodying some research work. If my lectures, I thought, were to contain nothing but new original work, they could be delivered only to a few advanced students of the Ancient Indian History and would hardly be understood by the people in general. If, on the other hand, they were to be such as would be intelligible to the latter, there was the danger of their being more popular than scholarly in character. Was it possible, I asked myself, to realise both the ends, *i.e.* to satisfy both the classes,—the scholars and the people? After thinking about the matter, I came to the conclusion that both the objects could be fulfilled if I selected a period and delivered my lectures on it. Perhaps the most neglected period was the one which immediately preceded the rise of the Mauryan power, although it was in some respects the most important one. This period was accordingly chosen and the lectures delivered. How far I have succeeded in interesting the specialists and the laymen in the subject-matter of these lectures I leave it to them to determine.

The most important event of the period I have selected, *viz*: from 650 to 325 B.C., is the completion of the Aryan colonisation of Southern India. This has, therefore, become the theme of my first lecture. In my second, I have dealt with the political history of the period, the characteristic feature of which is the gradual evolution of Imperialism. Shortly before Buddha, the Aryanised India had been divided into sixteen tiny States, mostly kingships, which by the process of centralisation were developed into four Monarchies when Buddha was living, and these Monarchies, again, culminated into Imperialism about a century after his demise. My Third and Fourth Lectures pertain to the Administrative History, a subject which has not yet attracted as much attention of the scholars as it deserves though the materials even now at our command are enough for the purpose. The Third Lecture is divided into two parts, the first of which deals with the Literature on Hindu Polity to which we are indebted for our knowledge of this subject. This, I am afraid, is more of an esoteric than of an exoteric character, and may, therefore, prove somewhat abstruse to the general reader. The second part (p. 114 and ff.) aims at setting forth some of the Hindu conceptions of Monarchy, and will, I hope, be read with some interest. Therein I have attempted to set forth the evidence which, if it is impartially and dispassionately considered, seems to show that there was a time in the Ancient

History of India when Monarchy was not absolute and uncontrolled. We have been so much accustomed to read and hear of Monarchy in India as being always and invariably unfettered and despotic that the above conclusion is apt to appear incredible to many as it no doubt was to me for a long time. In the Fourth Lecture I have endeavoured to show that Monarchy was not the only form of political government known to India and the governments of a more or less popular character such as oligarchy, aristocracy and democracy were also flourishing side by side with it. In this lecture I have also endeavoured to give a glimpse into the rules and regulations of debate which characterised the popular assemblies of Ancient India and have pointed out that they bear a remarkably close correspondence to those followed by the modern civilised age.

The Bengalis are a loving and lovable people, and many are the lecturers and teachers of the Calcutta University from whom I have received willing help and suggestions of various kinds. It is impossible to mention the names of them all here in this short preface. But I must mention the name of Mr. Narayan Chandra Banerji, M.A., for the invaluable assistance he rendered me in connection with my Lectures on the Administrative History before he formally became Lecturer of the University. The preparation of the Index is solely the work of my pupil Mr. N. G. Majumdar, B.A., who also helped me in revising the proofs.

It is scarcely necessary for me to add that the subject of the Ancient Indian History and Culture is a progressive one, and with every additional study and find of new materials some of the conclusions previously drawn are likely to be modified. And, as a matter of fact, as this book is reaching its completion, I myself am aware that I now hold somewhat different views on one or two matters dealt with in these Lectures. Similarly, though no effort has been spared to ensure accuracy and fullness, I do not expect this book to be by any means free from defects. But I request my readers not to play the role of a cattlelouse described in the well-known Sanskrit verse,* but rather to confine their attention to the good points only, if there be any, in these Lectures, and thus help to carry forward the torch of research work to illumine the dark periods of Ancient Indian History.

An outsider like myself has only to see the affairs of the Calcutta University and be convinced that the progress of the Ancient History of India or of Sanskrit, Pāli and Prākṛit studies is due solely to the solicitude and encouragement of one single person, and it is to this person, therefore, that this book has been dedicated. In the dedicatory pages will be found his portrait, which, I may add, was inserted much against his wishes.

D. R. B.

* The verse says that a cattle-louse, though it is perched on a cow's udder, will have her blood, not her milk.

ABBREVIATIONS

Aṅg. N.	... Aṅguttara-Nikāya.
ASI. AR.	... Archæological Survey of India, Annual Report.
ASIR. / ASR.	... Archæological Survey of India, Reports. By Cunningham.
ASS.	... Ānandāśrama Sanskrit Series, Poona.
ASSI	... Archæological Survey of Southern India.
BG.	... Bombay Gazetteer.
Bib. Ind.	... Bibliotheca Indica.
BSPS.	... Bombay Sanskrit and Prākrit Series.
BSS.	... Bombay Sanskrit Series.
CCIM.	... Catalogue of Coins in the Indian Museum, Calcutta. By V. A. Smith.
CII.	... Corpus Inscriptionum Indicarum.
EC.	... Epigraphia Carnatica. By L. Rice.
EHI.	... Early History of India. Third Edition. By V. A. Smith.
EI.	... Epigraphia Indica.
GOS.	... Gaekwad's Oriental Series.
HASL.	... History of Ancient Sanskrit Literature. By F. Max Müller.
IA.	... Indian Antiquary.

Jāt.	... Jātakas.
JBBRAS.	... Journal of the Bombay Branch of the Royal Asiatic Society.
JBORS.	... Journal of the Bihar and Orissa Research Society.
JRAS.	... Journal of the Royal Asiatic Society of Great Britain and Ireland.
Maj. N.	... Majjhima-Nikāya.
PR.—WC.	... Progress Report of the Archæological Survey, Western Circle.
PTS.	... Pāli Text Society.
Saṁ. N	... Saṁyutta-Nikāya.
SBB.	... Sacred Books of the Buddhists.
SBE.	... Sacred Books of the East.
TSS.	... Trivandrum Sanskrit Series.
VOJ.	... Vienna Oriental Journal.
VP.	... Vinaya Piṭaka.
ZDMG.	... Zeitschrift der Deuschen Morgeländischen Gesellschaft.

[All references to the Mahābhārata are from Pratapchandra Ray's edition.]

Lecture I.

Aryan Colonisation of Southern India and Ceylon.

I propose to open my first series of lectures as Carmichael Professor with the history of the pre-Maurya period, *i.e.* of the period extending from about 650 to 325 B.C. It is true that we do not know much about the political history of this period, but political history cannot be the whole history of any country. Again, it is the administrative, social, religious and ethnological history which is of much greater importance and far transcends political history in point of human interest and edification. And for the construction of this history for the period we have selected we have sufficient materials. We have works of the Sūtra period relating both to Law and Grammar. We have thus the *Dharma-śāstras* of Baudhāyana, Gautama, Āpastamba and so forth, and the *Ashṭādhyāyī* of Pāṇini and Kātyāyana's supplementary aphorisms or *vārtikas* on it. Further, it was prior to the rise of the Mauryas that Buddha lived and preached. And there is a general consensus of opinion among scholars that all the earlier works of the Buddhist Pāli canon were put together in the period to which we are confining ourselves. Let us, therefore, utilise these materials and try to see how India was socially, religiously and even politically from 650 to 325 B.C.

The principal characteristic of this period is the completion of the colonisation of Southern India and Ceylon by the Aryans; and this forms the subject of to-day's lecture. It is worthy of note that the southern half of India was called Dakshiṇāpatha, which means 'Road to the South'. Already in a Vedic hymn,[1] although it is one of the latest, we meet with an expression *dakshiṇā padā*, meaning 'with southward foot', and used with reference to a man who is expelled to the south. This cannot of course denote the *Dakshiṇāpatha* or Southern India as we understand it, but rather the country lying beyond the world then inhabited by the Aryans. It was in the Brāhmaṇa period, however, that they for the first time seem to have crossed the Vindhya range which separates the south from the north half of India. In the Aitareya Brāhmaṇa[2] *e.g.*, a prince named Bhīma is designated Vaidarbha, 'prince of Vidarbha'. This shows that the Aryans had come down below the Vindhyas and settled in Vidarbha or western Berars immediately to the south of this mountain range. The same Brāhmaṇa[3] represents the sage Viśvāmitra to

[1] *Rig-Veda* X. 61. 8.
[2] Vii. 34. 9.
[3] Vii. 17-18; also in *Śāṅkhāyana-Śrauta-Sūtra*, xv. 26.

have adopted Śunaḥśepa as his son and named him Devarāta, much to the annoyance of fifty of his sons, who in consequence were cursed by their father to "live on the borders" of the province then occupied by the Aryans. The descendants of these sons of Viśvāmitra's, the Brāhmaṇa further tells us, formed the greater bulk of the Dasyus and were variously known as Andhras, Puṇḍras, Śabaras, Pulindas and Mūtibas. Of these the Andhras, Pulindas and Śabaras at any rate are known from the Mahābhārata, Rāmāyaṇa and Purāṇas to have been tribes of Southern India; and though the exact provinces inhabited by them in the time of the Aitareya Brāhmaṇa cannot be definitely settled, it cannot for a moment be doubted that they lived to the south of the Vindhyas and that the Aryans had already come in contact with these non-Aryan peoples.

Let us now see what we learn from Pāṇini, the founder of the most renowned School of Grammar and who lived about 600 B.C. In his *sūtras* or grammatical aphorisms he shows an extensive knowledge of the ancient geography of India. Most of the countries, places and rivers mentioned by him are, of course, to be found in the Punjāb and Afghānistān. Belonging to India farther south he mentions Kachchha (IV.2.133), Avanti (IV.1.176), Kośala (IV.1.171) and Kaliṅga (IV.I.170).

But he makes no mention of any province to the south of the Narmadā except that of Aśmaka (IV.1.173). One of the oldest works of Pāli Buddhist literature, the *Sutta-nipāta*,[1] speaks of a Brāhmaṇ *guru* called Bāvarin as having left the Kosala country and settled near a village on the Godhāvarī in the Assaka (Aśmaka) territory in the Dakkiṇāpatha (Dakshiṇāpatha). The story tells us that Bāvarin sent his sixteen pupils to pay their homage to Buddha and confer with him. The route by which they proceeded northwards is also described.[2] First, they went to Patiṭṭhāna of the Muḷaka[3] country, then to Māhissatī, to Ujjenī, Gonaddha,[4] Vedisa and Vanasahvaya; to

---

[1] Vs. 976-7. [2] Ibid, Vs. 1011-3.

[3] In the text of the *Sutta-nipāta* edited by V. Fausboll, the reading *Aḷaka* is adopted (Vs.977 & 1011), and the variant *Muḷaka* noticed in the foot-notes. There can, however, be no doubt that Muḷaka must be the correct reading. We know of no country of the name Aḷaka. Muḷaka, on the other hand, is well-known. Thus in the celebrated Nāsik cave inscription of Vāsishṭhīputra Puḷumāvi, the Muḷaka country has been associated with Asaka (Aśmaka), exactly as it has been done in the *Sutta-nipāta* (EI., VIII.60). The same country seems to have been mentioned as Maulika by Varāhamihira in his *Bṛihat-saṁhitā* (XIV. 8.)

[4] Considering that Godāvarī has been called Godhāvarī in the *Sutta-nipāta*, Gonaddha can very well be taken to stand for Gonadda-Gonarda, the place from which Patañjali, author of the *Mahābhāshya*, hailed. Sir Ramkrishna Bhandarkar has shown on the authority of the *Mahābhāshya* that Sāketa was situated on the road from Gonarda to Pāṭaliputra (IA. II. 70). This is exactly in accordance with what the *Sutta-nipāta* says, for Sāketa, according to the route taken by Bāvarin's pupils was on the way from Gonaddha to the Magadha country. The native place of Patañjali was, therefore, in Central India somewhere between Ujjain and Besnagar near Bhilsā.

Kosambī, Sāketa and Sāvatthi (capital of the Kosala country); to Setavya, Kapilavatthu and Kusināra; to Pāvā, Vesālī (capital of Magadha), and finally to Pāsāṇaka Chetiya where Buddha then was. The description of this route is very important in more than one ways. In the first place, it will be seen that Bāvarin's settlement was much to the south of Patiṭṭhāna, *i.e.* Paiṭhaṇ in Nizam's territory, because Patiṭṭhāna was the principal town of the Muḷaka province, to the south of which was the Aśmaka country where Bāvarin then was. Secondly, it is worthy of note that Bāvarin's disciples went to North India straight through the Vindhyas. This disproves the theory of some scholars who hold that the Aryans were afraid of crossing the Vindhyas and went southwards to the Dekkan by an easterly detour round the mountain range.[1] After leaving Patiṭṭhāna or Paiṭhaṇ we find the party reaching Māhissatī, *i.e.* Māhishmatī, which has been correctly identified with Māndhātā on the Narmadā on the borders of the Indore State.[2] Evidently, Bāvarin's pupils must have passed to Māhishmatī, *i.e.* to the other side of the Vindhyas through the Vidarbha country.

Let us now turn to Pāṇini and the School of Grammar that he founded. We have seen that

---

[1] See *e.g.* *Early History of the Dekkan* (Second Edition), p. 9.

[2] JRAS., 1910, 445-6.

Aśmaka is the only country in the Dekkan, which he mentions. The case, however, is different with Kātyāyana who wrote aphorisms called *vārtikas* to explain and supplement Pāṇini and who has been assigned to the middle of the 4th century B.C. Now, to a Pāṇini's *sūtra* : *janapada—śabdāt kshatriyād=añ* (IV. 1. 168), Kātyāyana adds a *vārtika*, *Pāṇḍor=ḍyaṇ*, from which we obtain the form Pāṇḍya.[1] If this *vārtika* had not been made, we should have had the form not Pāṇḍya but Pāṇḍava. Again, we have a *sūtra* of Pāṇini, *Kambojāl=luk* (IV. 1. 175), which lays down that the word Kamboja denotes not only the Kamboja country or the Kamboja tribe but also the Kamboja king. But then there are other words which are exactly like Kamboja in this respect but which Pāṇini has not mentioned. Kātyāyana is, therefore, compelled to supplement the above *sūtra* with the *vārtika*, *Kambojādibhyo=lug–vachanaṁ Choḍādyartham*. This means that like Kamboja the words Choḍa, Kaḍera and Kerala denote each not only the

---

[1] I am not yet in a position to determine finally whether this is a *vārtika* of Kātyāyana or a supplement of Patañjali. Sir Ramkrishna Bhandarkar in his *Early History of the Dekkan* (p. 7. 8 n. 3) adopts the former view, whereas the text of Patañjali's *Mahābhāshya*, as edited by Kielhorn in the Bombay Sanskrit Series, inclines one to the latter view. Even if this last proves ultimately to be the correct view, this in no way vitiates my main conclusion, because as the Pāṇḍyas are referred to both by Megasthenes in his *Indika* and by Aśoka in his Rock Edicts,, their immigration to and settlement in South India were complete long before the rise of the Maurya power.

country and the tribe but also the king. It will thus be seen that Choḍa and Kerala, which are obviously countries situated in Southern India, were known to Kātyāyana, but not to Pāṇini. Of course, no sane scholar who has studied the *Ashṭādhyāyī* will be so bold as to assert that Pāṇini was a careless or ignorant grammarian. But we have not one word, but at least three words, *viz.* Pāṇḍya, Choḍa and Kerala, the formation of whose forms has not been explained by Pāṇini, which any accurate and thorough-going grammarian would have done if they had been known to him. The only legitimate conclusion that can, therefore, be drawn is that the names of these southern countries were not known to Pāṇini, or in other words, were not known to the Aryans in the seventh century B. C., but were known to them shortly before the middle of the fourth century B. C. when Kātyāyana lived. As regards Ceylon or Tāmraparṇi as it was called in ancient days, it was certainly known to the Aryans long before the rise of the Maurya power. It has been mentioned not only by Aśoka as Taṁbapaṇi in his Rock Edict XIII but also as Taprobane by Megasthenes,[1] who, as most of you are aware, was the ambassador sent by Seleukos Nicator of Syria to the court of Chandragupta, founder of the Maurya dynasty and grandfather of Aśoka. Contemporaneously with

[1] IA. VI. 129.

Megasthenes lived Kauṭilya, who in his *Artha-śāstra*[1] speaks of pearls being found among other places in the Tāmrapaṇi river, in Paṇḍya-kavāṭaka, and near the Mahendra mountain—all situated on the extremity of the Southern Peninsula.

Now, the name of one of these southern kingdoms was Choḍa, which was called Chōṛa in Tamiḷ and Choḷa in Telugu. The people also were called by the same name. I cannot resist the temptation of saying that it is from this Chō.a people that the Sanskrit word *chora* meaning a thief has been derived. An exactly analogous instance we have in the word Dasyu or Dāsa, which originally denoted the Dahae people of the Caspian Steppes[2] but which even in the Vedic period acquired a derogatory sense and soon after signified "a robber". If Dasyu thus originally was the name of a non-Aryan tribe and used in the sense of a robber, it is perfectly intelligible that the name of another non-Aryan people, *viz.* the Chōṛas, was similarly employed to express a similar meaning. And this seems to have been the case, because the Vedic terms

---

[1] p. 75. For the river Tāmraparṇi, see further in the sequel. It is also referred to in Aśoka's Rock Edict II. Kauṭilya's Pāṇḍya-kavāṭaka seems to be the same as Pāṇḍya-vāṭaka or Pāṇḍya-vāṭabhava of the *Bṛihat-saṁhitā* (80. 2 and 6). Mahendra here seems to be the most southerly spur of the Travancore Hills (JRAS., 1894, 262).

[2] Hillebrandt, *Vedische Mythologie*, I. 95; E. Kuhn's *Zeitschrift*, 28. 214.

for a thief are *taskara*, *tāyu*, *stena* and *paripanthin*, but never *chora*, this word being for the first time found in the Taittirīya Āraṇyaka [1] which is a late work. This conclusion is strengthened by the fact that in Latin and Greek also, there is no word, signifying "a thief," which corresponds to *chora* in sound.

The case, however, was different in regard to the name of the other people, *viz.* Pāṇḍya. Kātyāyana, we have seen, derives it from Pāṇḍu. This shows that the Pāṇḍyas were an Aryan tribe, and not an alien tribe like the Cholas or Choṛas. Now, a Greek writer called Pliny tells us a tradition about these Pāṇḍyas, on the authority of Megasthenes, that they were descended from Pandœa, the only daughter of the Indian Ḥercules, *i.e.*, of Kṛishṇa. She went away from the country of the Śaurasenas, whose principal towns were Methora or Mathurā and Cleisobora or Kṛishṇapura, and was assigned by her father just "that portion of India which lies southward and extends to the sea." [2] It is thus clear that the Pāṇḍyas were connected with the north and were an Aryan race. The account given by Megasthenes, however, like many traditions of this nature, is to be regarded as a combination of both truth and fiction. In the first place no authority from any epic or Purāṇa is forthcoming to show that Kṛishṇa had a

[1] X. 65.

[2] IA. VI 249-50 and 344.

daughter and of the name of Pāṇḍyā. Secondly, though Mathurā is connected with the infancy of Kṛishṇa, he lived as a ruler, not at Mathurā but at Dvārakā from where alone he could send his daughter. These are, therefore, the elements of fiction that got mixed up with the immigration of the Pāṇḍyas. What appears to be the truth is that there was a tribe called Pāṇḍu round about Mathurā, and that when a section of them went southwards and were settled there, they were called Pāṇḍyas. This is clear, I think, from Kātyāyana's *vārtika, Pāṇḍor-ḍyaṇ*, which means that the suffix *ya* was to be attached not to Pāṇḍu the name of the father of the Pāṇḍavas but to Pāṇḍu, which was the name of a Kshatriya tribe as well as of a country. Evidently Pāṇḍya denotes the descendants of the Pāṇḍu tribe, and must have been so called when they migrated southwards and established themselves there.[1] Nay, we have got evidence to show that there was a tribe called Pāṇḍu. Ptolemy, who wrote geography of India about A.D. 150, speaks not only of the kingdom of Pandion or Pāṇḍya but also of the country of the Pandoöuoi in the Punjāb.[2] These Pandoöuoi can be no other than the people Pāṇḍu. Again, Varāha-

---

[1] We also meet with similar *taddhita* forms in later history. Thus we have instances of early tribes being called Chalukya, Kadamba and so forth, whose descendants later on came to be called Chālukya, Kādamba and so on.

[2] IA., XIII. 331 and 349.

mihira, the celebrated astronomer, who flourished about the middle of the 6th century A.D., makes mention of a tribe called Pāṇḍus and places them in Madhyadeśa.[1] There can, therefore, be no doubt about the existence of a people called Pāṇḍus. And as according to Varāhamihira they were somewhere in the Madhyadeśa, it is quite possible that in the time of Megasthenes they were settled round about Mathurā? Megasthenes' statement that the Pāṇḍyas of the south were connected with the Jumna and Mathurā seems to be founded on fact, because the Greek writers, Pliny and Ptolemy, tell us that the capital of the Pāṇḍyas in the south was Modoura,[2] *i.e.*, Madurā, the principal town of the district of the same name in the Madras Presidency. The fact that the Pāṇḍyas of the south called their capital Madhurā clearly shows that they came from the north from some country whose capital was Mathurā and thus gives remarkable confirmation to what Megasthenes has told us. This is quite in accordance with the practice of the colonists naming the younger towns or provinces after the older.

We thus see that an Aryan tribe called Pāṇḍu went southwards, and occupied the southernmost part of the peninsula, where they were known as Pāṇḍya and their capital Madhurā

---

[1] *Bṛihat-saṁhitā*, XIV. 3.

[2] IA., XIII. 368.

or Mathurā. But the story of the migrations of this enterprising Aryan tribe does not end here. We have to note that there is a third Matura in Ceylon, and also a fourth Madura in the Eastern Archipelago.[1] The natural conclusion is that the Pāṇḍyas did not rest satisfied with occupying the extremest southern part of the peninsula, but went farther southward and colonised Ceylon also. For, as just stated, the Pāṇḍyas no doubt appear to have come from Mathurā, the capital of the Śaurasena country as told by Megasthenes, because this alone can explain why they gave the name Mathurā to the capital of their new kingdom situated at the south end of India. And the fact that we have another Mathurā in Ceylon shows that the Pāṇḍyas alone could go there and have a third capital of this name. Besides, as the Pāṇḍyas occupied the southern extremity of India, it was they who could naturally be expected to go and settle themselves in Ceylon. But they seem to have gone there, not from the Madurā but from the Tinnevelly District. I have told you that the ancient name of Ceylon was Tāmraparṇi, but we have to remember that Tāmraparṇi was the name of a river also.[2] This doubtless is the present river

---

[1] Caldwell, *Grammar of the Dravidian Languages*, Intro., p. 16.

[2] Mahābhārata III. 88. 15. That the Pāṇḍyas held the Madurā District is quite certain, because it was the territory immediately round about Madhurā, their capital. That they held also the Tinnevelly

Tāmraparṇi in the Tinnevelly District. Scholars have no doubt tacitly admitted that there was a connection somehow between this river and Ceylon, but this connection can be rendered intelligible only on the supposition that the Tinnevelly District was called Tāmraparṇi after the river, just as Sindhu or Sind was after the river Sindhu or Indus. In that case it is intelligible that when the Pāṇḍyas went to Ceylon, they named it Tāmraparṇi after the country they left. Again, coming as they did from the Tinnevelly District they would naturally land in the north-western part of the Island. And it is quite in keeping with this supposition that we find the ancient civilised and populous district of Ceylon, the so-called Kalah located, not in the south, east or north-east, but north-west part of the Island. [1]

Let us now see how the Aryan colonisation of Southern India must have been accomplished. We know that when the Aryans migrated in ancient times from Afghānistān and Punjāb to the different parts of Northern India, they did

District is clear from what Ptolemy and the author of the Periplus tell us about the Pāṇḍya kingdom (IA., XIII. 331). Northwards their rule seems to have extended as far as the highlands in the neighbourhood of the Coimbatore gap. Its western boundary was formed by the southern range of the Ghāṭs. That the Aryans had occupied the Tinnevelly District at this time is evident from the fact that we have here not only the sacred river Tāmraparṇi but also the sacred place Agastya-tīrtha—both mentioned in the Mahābhārata.

[1] *Jour. Ceylon Br. R.A. Soc.*, VII. 57 & ff.

so under the leadership of the Kshatriya tribes, and hence their new settlements were called after the names of those tribes. A curious legend in this connection is worth quoting from the Śatapatha-Brāhmaṇa, from which it would appear that when the Aryans pushed forward to the east of the Sarasvatī, they were led by Māthava the Videgha, and his priest.[1] They went at first as far east as the Sadānīrā which formed the boundary between Kośala and Videha and which therefore corresponds to the Little Gaṇḍak of the present day.[2] For some time they did not venture to cross this river. They did however cross it, and, at the time when the Śatapatha-Brāhmaṇa was composed, were settled to the east of it in a province called Videha no doubt after the name of the tribe to which the king Māthava belonged. Nay, we have got Pāṇini's authority to that effect; thus, according to him, *Pañchālānāṁ nivāso janapadaḥ Pāñchālaḥ*, *i.e.* the word *Pāñchālaḥ* denotes the country or kingdom which the Kshatriya tribe Pañchāla occupied. What happened in North India must have happened in South India also. I have already referred to the tribe Pāṇḍu who were settled in the southernmost part of India and after whom it was called Pāṇḍya. This was certainly a

---

[1] SBE., XII. Intro. xli seq.: 104 seq.

[2] JRAS., 1907, p. 644.

Kshatriya tribe. Again, we have a passage in Kauṭilya's *Arthaśāstra, viz. Dāṇḍakyo nāma Bhojaḥ kāmāt Brāhmaṇa-kanyām=abhimanyamānas=sa-bandhu-rāshṭro vinanāśa* (a Bhoja known as Dāṇḍakya or king of Daṇḍakā, making a lascivous attempt on a Brāhmaṇ girl, perished along with his relations and kingdom.)[1] Bhoja was, of course, the name of a Kshatriya tribe, as we know from the Mahābhārata and Harivaṁśa.[2] And a prince of this tribe is here said to have been a ruler of Daṇḍakā, which is another name for Mahārāshṭra.[3] As all the incidents which Kauṭilya mentions along with that of Dāṇḍakya Bhoja took place long before his time and as he himself was, we know, the prime-minister of Chandragupta, founder of the Maurya dynasty, and consequently lived at the close of the fourth century B.C., it appears that the Bhojas must have taken possession of Mahārāshṭra, at least in the fifth century B.C., if not earlier. I have already told you that the Buddhist work *Suttanipāta* speaks of Patiṭṭhāna or Paiṭhaṇ in Nizam's Dominions. But there was an older Patiṭṭhāna or Pratishṭhāna on the confluence of the Ganges and the Jumnā, which was the

---

[1] *Kauṭilīyaṁ Arthaśāstraṁ* (Bibliotheca Sanskrita—No. 37), p. 11.

[2] *Mahābhārata*, I. 85.34, II. 14. 6, & VI. 9. 40; *Harivaṁśa*, 1895, 8816, 12838.

[3] R. G. Bhandarkar, *Early History of the Dekkan*, p. 4.

capital of Aila Purūravas.[1] The practice of naming the younger town after the older one is universal, and is well-known even in the colonies of European nations. I have already quoted you an instance from India, *viz.* of Mathurā. And Pratishṭhāna is but another instance. It thus seems that on the bank of the Godāvarī we had a colony from the country of of which the older Pratishṭhāna was the capital, and it is probable that we had here a colony of the Aila tribe.[2] Even as late as the third century A.D., we find North Indian Aryan tribes or families going southwards and settling themselves somewhere in Southern India. A Buddhist *stūpa* has been discovered at Jagayyapeṭa in the Kistnā District, Madras. We have got here at least three inscriptions of this period which refer themselves to the reign of the king Māḍharīputra Śrī-Vīrapurushadatta of the Ikshvāku family.[3] This indicates that the Kistnā and adjoining Districts were held in the third century A.D. by the Ikshvākus,[4]

---

[1] Wilson, *Vishṇu-Purāṇa*, III. 237; *Vikramorvaśīyam* (BSPS. Ed.), p. 41; believed to be present Jhusi opposite Allahabad fort.

[2] In the Mahābhārata are mentioned both Ailavaṁśa (I. 94. 65) and Aila-vaṁśyas (II. 14. 4). Ailas are mentioned also in the Purāṇas.

[3] Lüders, *List of Brāhmī Inscriptions etc*, Nos. 1202-4.

[4] It is not at all unlikely that Māḍharīputra Śrī-Vīrapurushadatta was a prince of Dakshiṇa-Kosala which in the third century A.D. may have extended as far as the east coast. We know that Uttara-Kosala, with its capital of Sāketa or Ayodhyā, was ruled over by the Ikshvākus,

who certainly must have come from the north. We know that Rāma, the hero of the Rāmāyaṇa, belonged to the Ikshvāku race. So did Buddha, the founder of Buddhism. The Ikshvākus are also mentioned in the Purāṇas as a historical royal dynasty ruling in North India. The Ikshvākus of the Kistnā District must, therefore, have come from the north.

It is true that the Aryan civilisation was thus to a certain extent spread over Southern India through conquest. But this cannot be the whole cause. Causes of a pacific and more important nature must also have operated. We are so much accustomed to hear about the enterprising and prosylitising spirit of the Buddhist and Jaina monks that we are apt to think that Brahmanism had never shown any missionary zeal. Is this, however, a fact? Did not the Brāhmaṇs or at any rate any of the hymn-composing families put forth any missionary effort and help in the dissemination of the Aryan culture? I cannot help thinking that the ancient Ṛishis were not mere passive inert thinkers, but were active though not aggressive propagators of their faith? Tradi-

---

and it seems that when the Ikshvākus spread themselves southwards, their new province also was called Kosala, *dakshiṇa* being also applied to it to distinguish it from their original territory which therefore became Uttara-Kosala. (Dakshiṇa—) Kosala was certainly well-known in the fourth century A.D., as it is mentioned in the Allāhābād pillar inscription of Samudragupta and included in Dakshiṇāpatha.

tion, narrated in the Mahābhārata and Rāmāyaṇa, says that it was the Brāhmaṇ sage Agastya who first crossed the Vindhya range and led the way to the Aryan immigration.[1] When Rāma began his southward march and was at Pañchavaṭī, Agastya was already to the south of the Vindhyas and was staying in a hermitage about two *yojanas* from it. This is not all. We find him evermore penetrating farther and farther into the hitherto unknown south, and civilising the Dravidians. Nay, this is admitted by the Tamiḷ people themselves. They make Agastya the founder of their language and literature and call him by way of eminence the *Tamiẓmuni* or Tamilian sage. They still point to a mountain in the Tinnevelly District, which is commonly called by the English Agastier,—*i.e.* Agastya's hill—"Agastya being supposed to have finally retired thither from the world after civilising the Dravidians."[2] I am not unaware that these are legends. It is, however, a mistake to suppose that legends teach us nothing historical. It may very well be doubted whether Agastya as he figures in these legends is a historical personality. But a man is certainly lacking the historical sense if he cannot read in these legends the historical truth that Ṛishis took a most prominent but

---

[1] *Mahābhārata*, III. 104; *Rāmāyaṇa* III. 11. 85.

[2] Caldwell, *Grammar of the Dravidian Languages*, Intro., 101, 119.

unobtrusive part in the Aryan colonisation and the diffusion of Aryan culture. The old Ṛishis of India, I think, were as enthusiastic and enterprising in this respect as the Buddhist and Jaina missionaries, and were often migrating with their host of pupils to distant countries. I shall take only one instance. I hope you remember the Brāhmaṇ *guru* Bāvarin, whom I mentioned a few minutes ago. His story appears in the *Sutta-Nipāta*. He is described therein as perfect in the three Vedas. He has sixteen disciples—all Brāhmaṇs, and each one of them again had his host of pupils. They all bore matted hair and sacred skins, and are styled Ṛishis. With these pupils of his and their pupils' pupils Bāvarin was settled on the bank of the Godāvarī in the Aśmaka territory, where he performed a sacrifice. He was thus settled on the confines of the Dakshiṇāpatha, as it was then known, if not beyond. And yet we are told that originally he was at Śrāvastī, capital of the Kośala country. He and his pupils had thus traversed at least 600 miles before they came and were settled on the Godāvarī. It will thus be seen that the Ṛishis were in the habit of moving in large numbers and to long distances, and making their settlements where they performed sacrifices. This is exactly in keeping with what we gather from the Rāmāyaṇa. To the south of the Vindhya, we learn, there were many Brāhmaṇ anchorites who lived in hermitages at different places and performed their sacrifices before Rāma penetrated Daṇḍakāraṇya and commenced his career of conquest. There was an aboriginal tribe called the Rākshasas who disturbed the sacrifices and devoured the hermits and thus placed themselves in hostile opposition to the Brahmanical institutions. On the other hand, under the designation of Vānaras, we have got another class of aborigines, who allied themselves to the Brāhmaṇs and embraced their form of religious worship. Even among the Rākshasas we know we had an exception in Vibhīshaṇa, brother of Rāvaṇa, who is said to be *na tu Rākshasa-cheshṭitaḥ*,[1] not behaving himself like a Rākshasa. This was the state of things in Southern India when Rāma came there. This clearly shows that the Ṛishis were always to the forefront in the work of colonising Southern India and introducing Aryan civilisation. Amongst them Agastya was the only Ṛishi, who fought with the Rākshasas and killed them. The other Ṛishis, like true missionaries, never resorted to the practice of retaliation, though they believed rightly or wrongly that they had the power of ridding themselves of their enemy. One of them distinctly says to Rāma : *Kāmaṁ tapaḥ-prabhāveṇa śaktā hantum niśācharān chirārjitaṁ na ch-echchhāmas-*

[1] *Rāmāyaṇa*, III. 17. 22.

tapaḥ khaṇḍayituṁ vayaṁ: "It is true that by the power of our austerities we could at will slay these goblins; but we are unwilling to nullify (the merit of) our austerities."[1] And it was simply because through genuine missionary spirit the Ṛishis refused to practice retaliation that Rāma, like a true Kshatriya, intervened and waged war with the Rākshasas. This high noble spirit of the ancient Ṛishis, manifested in their mixing with the aborigines and civilising them, is not seen from the Rāmāyaṇa only. It may also be seen from the story of the fifty of Viśvāmitra's sons, mentioned in the Aitareya Brāhmaṇa and referred to at the beginning of this lecture. They strongly disapproved of his adoption of Śunaḥśepa, and were for that reason cursed by Viśvāmitra to live on the borders of the Aryan settlements. And their progeny, we are told, are the Andhras, Puṇḍras, Śabaras and so forth. If we read the legend aright, it clearly indicates that even the scions of such an illustrious hymn-composing family as that of Viśvāmitra migrated southward boldly, and what is more, married and mixed freely with the aborigines, with the object of diffusing Aryan culture amongst them.

But by what routes did the Aryans penetrate South India? This question we have now to consider. The main route, I think, is the reverse

[1] *Ibid.*, III. 10. 13-14.

of the one by which Bāvarin's pupils went to Magadha from Aśmaka. This was described a short time ago. The Aryan route thus seems to have lain through the Avanti country, the southernmost town of which was Māhissatī or Māndhātā on the Narmadā, from where the Aryans crossed the Vindhyas and penetrated Southern India. They began by colonising Vidarbha from which they proceeded southwards first to the Muḷaka territory with its principal town Patiṭṭhāna or Paiṭhaṇ and from there to the Aśmaka country. By what route farther southward they immigrated is not clear, but the find-spots of Aśoka's inscriptions perhaps afford a clue. One copy of his Minor Rock Edicts has been found at Maski in the Lingsugur Taluq of the Raichur District, Nizām's Dominions, [1] and three more farther southward, in the Chitaldrug District of the Mysore State. [2] A few Jaina cave inscriptions have come to light also in the Madurā District [3] and appear to belong to the second century B.C. and possibly earlier. As Aśoka's edicts and these cave inscriptions are in Pāli, these certainly were the districts colonised by the Aryans. The Aryans thus seem to to have gone south from the Aśmaka territory through the modern Raichur and Chitaldrug

[1] *Hyderabad Archaeological Series*, No. I, p. 1.

[2] EC., Vol. XI. (Intro.), p. 2.

[3] *Annual Report* on Epigraphy for the year ending 31st March 1912, p. 57.

Districts, from where they must have gone to the Madurā District which was originally in the Pāṇḍya kingdom. This seems to agree with the tradition of their immigration preserved among the Tamiḷ Brāhmaṇs. These Brāhmaṇs have a section called Bṛihachcharaṇa which means the Great Immigration, and must refer to a large southward movement [1]. They are subdivided into Mazhnāḍu and Molagu. The Mazhnāḍu sub-section is further divided into Kandra-māṇikkam, Mangudi and Sathia-mangalam etc., all villages along the Western Ghāṭs—showing that in their southward movement they clung to the highlands and peopled the skirts of the present province of Mysore and the Coimbatore and Madurā Districts— a conclusion which agrees with that just drawn from the find-spots of the Aśoka and Cave Inscriptions in Southern India.

Another route by which the Aryans seem to have gone to South India was by the sea. They appear to have sailed from the Indus to Kachchha, and from there by sea-coast to Surāshṭra or Kāṭhiāwāṛ, from Kāṭhiāwāṛ to Bharukachchha or modern Broach, and from Bharukachchha to Suppāraka or Sopārā in the Ṭhāṇā District of the Bombay Presidency. Baudhāyana, the author of a *Dharmaśāstra* quotes a verse from the Bhāllavin School of Law, which tells us

---

[1] IA., 1912, 231-2.

that the inhabitants of Sindhu, Sauvīra and Surāshṭra like those of the Dekkan were of mixed origin. This shows that the Aryans had begun colonising those parts. Towards the end of the period we have selected they seem to have advanced as far south as Sopārā. But as already stated they must have gone by the sea-route, because it is quite clear that no mention is traceable of any inland countries or towns between the sea-coast and the Dekkan. [1]

Now, wherever in India and Ceylon the Aryans penetrated, they introduced not only their civilisation, *i.e.* their religion, culture and and social organisation, but also imposed their language on the aborigines. It is scarcely necessary for me to expatiate on the former point, for it is an indisputable fact that the Hindu civilisation that we see everywhere in India or Ceylon is essentially Aryan. You know about it as much and as well as I do. This point, therefore, calls for no remarks. In regard to the Aryan language, however, I cannot do better than quote the following opinion of Sir George Grierson, an eminent linguist of the present day. "When an Aryan tongue,"

---

[1] It will be stated further on in the text that no less than three Buddhist *stūpas* have been found in the Kistnā District with quite a number of Pāli inscriptions showing that the Aryans had colonised that part. The question arises from where did the Aryans go there; They must have gone either from Kaliṅga or Aśmaka, most probably from the latter. See note on p. 40 below.

says he, "comes into contact with an uncivilized aboriginal one, it is invariably the latter which goes to the wall. The Aryan does not attempt to speak it, and the necessities of intercourse compelled the aborigine to use a broken 'pigeon' form of the language of a superior civilisation. As generations pass this mixed jargon more and more approximates to its model, and in process of time the old aboriginal language is forgotten and dies a natural death."[1] I completely endorse this view of Sir George Grierson except in one respect. This exception, you will at once see, is the Dravidian languages which are at present spoken in Southern India. It is, indeed, strange how the Aryan, failed to supplant the Dravidian, speech in this part of India, though it most successfully did in Northern India, where I have no doubt the Dravidian tongue prevailed before the advent of the Aryans. This will be seen from the fact that "Brahuī, the language of the mountaineers in the Khanship of Kelat in Beluchistan, contains not only some Dravidian words, but a considerable infusion of distinctively Dravidian forms and idioms"[2]. The discovery of this Dravidian element in a language spoken beyond the Indus tends to show that the Dravidians, like the Aryans, the Scythians, and so forth, must have

---

[1] *Imperial Gazetteer of India*, Vol. I. pp. 351-2.

[2] Caldwell, *Grammar of the Dravidian Languages*, Intro. pp. 43-4.

entered India by the north-western route. It is also a well-known fact, accepted by all scholars, that there are many Sanskrit words, which are really Dravidian, and Kittel, in his Kannaḍa-English Dictionary, gives a long list of them. But in compiling this list he seems to have drawn exclusively upon classical Sanskrit, which was never a *bhāshā* or spoken language. At least one Dravidian word, however, is known from the Vedic literature, which is admitted to be composed in the language actually spoken by the people. The word I mean is *maṭachī* which occurs in the Chhāndogya-Upanishad (I.10.1) in the passage *Maṭachī-hateshu Kurushu āṭikyā saha jāyayā Ushastir=ha Chākrāyaṇa ibhya-grāme pradrāṇaka uvāsa.* Here evidently the devastation of the crops in the Kuru country by *maṭachī* is spoken of. All the commentators except one have wrongly taken *maṭachī* to mean 'hailstones', but one commentator who is an exception rightly gives *rakta-varṇāḥ kshudra-pakshi-viśeshāḥ* as an alternative equivalent [1]. This shows that these "red-coloured winged creatures" can be no other than locusts, and that it is they which laid waste the fields of the Kuru country as they do to the present day in every part of India. It is interesting to note that this explanation of the commentator is confirmed by the fact that *maṭachī* is

[1] JRAS., 1911, p. 510.

a Sanskritised form of the well-known Canarese word *miḍiche* which is explained by Kittel's Dictionary as "a grasshopper, a locust" and which is used in this sense to this day in the Dhārwār District of the Bombay Presidency [1]. Scholars are unanimous on the point that the Chhāndogya-Upanishad is one of the earliest of the Upanishads. Nobody doubts that this Upanishad was put together in the North of India, especially in the Punjāb, and that the Sanskrit language in which it is composed represents the current speech of the day. And yet we find in it a term which is a genuinely Dravidian word. I have no doubt that more such will be forthcoming from the Vedic literature if scholars of the Dravidian languages undertake this task. And this will confirm the conclusion that the Dravidian tongue was prevalent in North India before the Aryans came and occupied it. The same conclusion is forced upon us by an examination of the vernaculars of North India. Take Bengali, for instance; the words *Khokā* and *Khukī* which mean 'boy' and 'girl' in Bengali are nothing but the Oraon *Kokā* and *Kokī*. The Bengali *telo*, 'head', is the Telugu *tā-lā* and Tamiḷ *Tā-lai*. *Nolā*, 'tongue' is Tamiḷ *nālu*. The plural suffix *gul* is used in Tamiḷ to denote 'many'. *Gulī* and *gulā* are used for the same

---

[1] IA., 1913, p. 235.

purpose in Bengali. Instances can be multiplied[1], but those given are enough, to show that even the vernacular Bengali, which bristles with Sanskrit and derivative words, is indebted to Dravidian languages for a pretty large portion of its vocabulary and structural peculiarities. What is strange is that even in Hindī speech Dravidian words have been traced. Even the commonest Hindī words *jhagṛā*, *āṭā* and so forth have been traced to Dravidian vocables[2]. No. reasonable doubt can therefore be entertained as to the Dravidian speech once being spoken in North India.

We thus see that the Dravidian tongue was once spoken in North India but was superseded by the Aryan, when the Aryans penetrated and established themselves there. It, therefore, becomes extremely curious how in Southern India the Aryan speech was not able to supplant the Dravidian. But here a question arises: Is it a fact that even in that part of the country no Aryan tongue was ever known or spoken by the aborigine, after the Aryans came and were settled here? I take my stand on epigraphic records as they alone can afford irrefragible evidence on the subject. Let us first take the

---

[1] For a detailed consideration of this subject, see *Bāṅgālābhāshāy Drāviḍī upādāna* by Mr. B. C. Mazumdar printed in *Sāhitya-parishat-patrikā*, Vol. XX. Pt. I.

[2] IA. 1916, p. 16.

province whose vernacular at present is Telugu. The earliest inscriptions found here are those of Aśoka. Evidently I mean the version of his Fourteen Rock Edicts engraved at Jaugaḍā in the Ganjām District, the extreme north-east part of the Madras Presidency. But I am afraid I cannot lay much stress upon it, because though Telugu is no doubt spoken in this district, Uṛiyā is not unknown here, at any rate in the northern portion of it. And it is a well-known fact that in a province where the ranges of any two languages or dialects meet, the boundary which divides one from the other is never permanently fixed, but is always changing. I shall not, therefore, refer here to the Fourteen Rock Edicts discovered in the Ganjām District, but shall come down a little southwards and select that district where none but a Dravidian language is spoken—I mean the Kistnā District. Here no less than three Buddhist *stūpa*s have been discovered, along with a number of inscriptions. The earliest of these is that at Bhaṭṭiproḷu, the next is the celebrated one at Amrāvatī, and the third is that at Jagayyapeṭa. The inscriptions connected with these monuments are short donative records, specifying each the name and social status of the donor along with the nature of his gift. An examination of these records shows that people of various classes and statuses participated in this series of religious benefactions. We will here leave aside the big folk, such as those who belonged to the warrior or merchant class, and who, it might be contended, were the Aryan conquerors. We will also leave aside the monks and nuns, because their original social status is never mentioned in Buddhist inscriptional records. We have thus left for our consideration the people who are called *herañika* or goldsmiths, and, above all, the *chammakāras* or leather-workers. These at any rate cannot be reasonably supposed to form part of the Aryan people who were settled in the Kistnā District, and yet we find that their names are clearly Aryan, showing that they imbibed the Aryan civilisation even to the extent of adopting their names. Thus, we have a goldsmith of the name of Sidhatha or Siddhārtha, two leather-workers (father and son) of the name of Vidhika or Vṛiddhika and Nāga.[1] All these unmistakably are Aryan names. but this string of names does not stop here. We have yet to make mention of another individual who is named Kanha or Kṛishṇa. This too is an Aryan name, but the individual, it is worthy of note, calls himself Damila,[2] which is exactly the same as Tamiḷ or Sanskrit Draviḍa. And, in fact, this is the earliest word so far found signifying the Dravidian race. We thus see that as the result

[1] ASSI., I. 91 & 102-3. [2] *Ibid.*, 104.

of the Aryan settlement in the Kistnā District, the local people were so steeped in Aryan civilisation that they went even to the length of taking Aryan proper names to themselves. But could they understand or speak the Aryan tongue? Do the inscriptions found in the Kistnā District throw any light on this point? Yes, they do, because the language of these records is Pāli,[1] and Pāli we know is an Aryan speech. This clearly proves that an Aryan tongue was spoken in the Kistnā District from at least 150 B.C. to 200 A.D.—the period to which the inscriptions belong. I am aware it is possible to argue that this Aryan language was spoken only by the Aryans who were settled there, and not necessarily by the people in general, and, above all, the lower classes. This argument is not convincing, because it is inconceivable that earlier Buddhism, whose one aim was to be in direct touch with the masses, and which must have obtained almost all its converts of this district from all sorts and conditions of the indigenous people including the lowest classes, could adopt an Aryan tongue unless it was at least as well known to and actually spoken by the people in general as their home tongue. This inference is confirmed by the fact that

[1] I use this term in the sense in which it has been taken by Mr. Francke in his *Pali and Sanskrit*. Perhaps this should have been styled monumental Pāli to distinguish it from literary Pāli, i.e. the Pāli of the Buddhist scriptures.

three copies of what are called Aśoka's Minor Rock Edicts have been found in the Chitaldrug District of the Mysore State,[1] *i.e.* in the very heart of what is now the Canarese-speaking province. One of these edicts enumerates the different virtues that constitute what Aśoka meant by *dhamma*, and the other exhorts all people especially those of low position to put forth strenuous endeavour after the highest life. All the inscriptions of Aśoka, especially these Edicts, had a very practical object in view. They were intended to be understood and pondered over by people of all classes, and as the language of these epigraphic records is Pāli, the conclusion is irresistible that though perhaps it was not the home tongue, it could be spoken, at least well understood, by all people including the lower classes. But this is not all. We have got incontestable evidence that up to the 4th century A.D., Pāli was also the official language of the kings even in those provinces where Dravidian languages are now suprem e. At least one stone inscription and five copper-plate charters have been found in these provinces, ranging from the second to the fourth or fifth century A.D. The stone inscription was found at Maḷavaḷḷi in Shimogā District, Mysore State.[2] It registers some grant to the god Maḷapaḷi by Viṇhukaḍa

[1] EC., XI. Intro. 1 & ff.

[2] Lüders, *List of Brāhmī Inscriptions*, Nos. 1195-6.

Chuṭukalānaṁda [1] Śātakarṇi of the Kadamba dynasty [2] who calls himself king of Vaijayantī, and records the renewal of the same grant by his son. Vaijayantī, we know, is Banavāsī in the North Kanara District, Bombay Presidency. At Banavāsī, too, we have found an inscription of the queen of this king. Both Banavāsī and Maḷavaḷḷi are situated in the Canarese-speaking country, and yet we find that the official language here is Pāli. The same conclusion is proved with reference to the Tamiḷ-speaking country by the five copper-plate grants referred to above. Of these five three belong to the Pallava dynasty reigning at Kāñchīpura, one to a king called Jayavarman, and one to Vijayadevavarman. [3]

---

[1] I had occasion to examine coins of two princes of this dynasty found in the North Canara District, Bombay. Their names on them are clearly Chuṭukalānaṁda and Mulānaṁda (PR.—WC., 1911-2, p. 5, para 18.) Prof. Rapson is inclined to take Chuṭu and Muḍa (Muṇḍa) as dynastic names (*Catalogue of the coins of the Andhra Dynasty* etc., Intro. lxxxiv-lxxxvi). In my opinion, the whole Chuṭuka(ku)lānaṁda and Mulānaṁda are proper names or individual epithets, for to me it is inconceivable how they could mention their dynastic names only on the coins and not individual names or epithets at all.

[2] Prof. Rapson has conclusively shown that Viṇhukaḍa Chuṭukalānaṁda and Śivaskandavarman of the Maḷavaḷḷi inscriptions were related to each other as father and son (*ibid*, liv-lv). But then it is worthy of note that the latter has been called king of the Kadambas in one of these records. It thus appears that both father and son belonged to the Kadamba dynasty—a conclusion which thoroughly agrees with the fact that their title *Vaijayantī-pura-rāja*, *Mānavya-sagotta* and *Hāritīputta* are exactly those of the Kadambas known to us from their copper-plate charters (*Bombay Gazetteer*, Vol. I., pt. II, p. 287).

[3] Lüders' *List*, Nos. 1200, 1205, 1327, 1328 and 1194.

The very fact that every one of these is a title-deed and has been drawn up in Pāli shows that this Aryan language must have been known to officials of even the lowest rank and also to literate and even semi-literate people. One of the three Pallava charters, *e.g.*, issues instructions, for the maintenance of the grant therein registered, not only to *rājakumāra* or royal princes, *senāpati* or generals, and so forth, but also to the free-holders of various villages (*gāmāgāma-bhojaka*), guards (*ārakhādhikata*) and even cowherds (*go-vallava*) who were employed in the king's service. The princes [1] and generals may perhaps be presumed to be of the Aryan stock and consequently speaking an Aryan tongue, but the free-holders of the various villages, guards and cowherds, at any rate, must be supposed to be of non-Aryan race. And when instructions are issued to them by a charter couched in Pāli, the conclusion is inevitable that this Aryan tongue, at least up to the fourth century A.D., was spoken and understood by all classes of people in a country of which the capital was Kāñchīpura or Conjeveram and which was and is now a centre of the Tamil language and literature.

Just now I have many a time remarked that Pāli might not have been the home tongue of the

[1] Personally I think most of the princes in Southern India were f Dravidian blood, as is clearly evidenced by their names such as Puḷumāvi, Viḷivāyakura, Kaḷalāya, Chuṭukala and so forth.

people but was well understood by them. Perhaps some of you would like to know what I exactly mean by this. I shall explain myself by giving an instance. We know that there are many Canarese-speaking districts which were conquered and held by the Marāṭhās. Some of them still belong to the Marāṭhā Chiefs. If you go to any one of these districts, you will find that although the indigenous people speak Canarese at home and among themselves, Marāṭhī is understood by many of them and even by some of the lower classes. This is the result of the Marāṭhā domination extending over only two centuries, and has happened notwithstanding the fact that the Canarese people have their own art and literature. As the Pāli inscriptions referred to above show, the Aryans had established themselves in Southern India for at least seven centuries. It is, therefore, no wonder that the Aryan tongue could be spoken, at any rate well understood, by the original Dravidians even to the lowest classes, as is clearly evidenced, I think, at least by the inscriptions of Aśoka and those connected with Buddhist *stūpas*. We must not, however, lose sight of the fact that the Aryan language for some reason or another had not become the home tongue of these Dravidians. Evidence in support of this conclusion, curiously enough, is forthcoming from an extraneous and unforeseen quarter. A papyrus of the second century A.D. was discovered in 1903 at Oxyrhynchus in Egypt, containing a Greek farce by an unknown author.[1] The farce is concerned with a Greek lady named Charition, who has been stranded on the coast of a country bordering the Indian Ocean. The king of this country addresses his retinue as "Chiefs of the Indians." In some places the same king and his countrymen use their own language especially when Charition has wine served to them to make them drunk. Many stray words have been traced, but so far only two sentences have been read, and these leave no doubt whatever as to their language having been Canarese. One of the sentences referred to his *bēre Koñcha madhu pātrakke hāki,* which means "having poured a little wine into the cup separately." The other sentence is *pānam bēr etti Kaṭṭi madhuvaṁ ber ettuvenu,* which means "having taken up the cup separately and having covered (it), I shall take wine separately." From the fact that the Indian language employed in the papyrus is Canarese, it follows that the scene of Charition's adventures is one of the numerous small ports on the western coast of India between Kārwār and Mangalore and that Canarese was at least imperfectly understood in that part of Egypt where the farce was composed and acted, for if the Greek

[1] JRAS., 1904, p. 399 ff.

audience in Egypt did not understand even a bit of Canarese, the scene of the drinking bout would be denuded of all its humour and would be entirely out of place. There were commercial relations of an intimate nature between Egypt and the west coast of India in the early centuries of the Christian era, and it is not strange if some people of Egypt understood Canarese. To come to our point, the papyrus clearly shows that, in the second century A.D., Canarese was spoken in Southern India even by princes, who most probably were Dravidian by extraction. The Canarese, however, which they spoke, was not pure Canarese, but was strongly tinctured with Aryan words. I have quoted two Canarese sentences from the Greek farce, and you will have seen that they contain the words *pātra* (cup), *pānaṁ* (drink) and *madhu* (wine), which are genuine Aryan vocables as they are to be found in the Vedas. The very fact that even in respect of ordinary affairs relating to drinking we find them using, not words of their home language as we would naturally expect them to do, but words from Aryan vocabulary, indicates what hold the Aryan speech had on their tongue.

Nevertheless it must be confessed that even seven centuries of Aryan domination in South India was not enough for the eradication of the Dravidian languages. It would be exceedingly interesting to investigate the circumstances which precluded the Aryan tongue here from supplanting the aboriginal one. Such an inquiry, I am afraid, is irrelevant here. And I, therefore, leave it to the Dravidian scholars to tackle this most interesting but also most bewildering problem.[1]

Though the causes that led to the preservation and survival of the Dravidian languages are not known at present, this much is certain, as I have shown above, that up till 400 A.D. at any rate, an Aryan tongue was spoken and known to the people in general just in those provinces where the Dravidian languages are now the only vernaculars. If such was the case, we can easily understand why in Ceylon to the present day we have an Indo-Aryan vernacular. For we have seen that the tide of the Aryan colonisation did not stop till it reached Ceylon. Naturally, therefore, not only the Aryan civilisation but also the Aryan speech was implanted from South India into this country, where, however, as in North India, it succeeded in completely superseding the tongue originally spoken there. This satisfactorily answers, I think, the question about the origin of Pāli in which the Buddhist scriptures

[1] Let me say here that the exact question to be answered is why the Dravidian, was supplanted by the Aryan, language in North India, but not in South India, although Aryan civilisation had apparently permeated South India as much as North India.

of Ceylon have been written. The Island was converted to Buddhism about the middle of the third century B. C. by the preaching of Mahinda, a son of the great Buddhist Emperor Aśoka. Naturally, therefore, the scriptures which Mahinda brought with him from his father's capital must have been in Māgadhī, the dialect of the Magadha country. As a matter of fact, however, the language of these scriptures, as we have them now, is anything but Māgadhī, though, of course, a few Magadhisms are here and there traceable. This discrepancy has been variously explained by scholars. Prof. Kern holds that Pāli was never spoken and was an artificial language altogether—a view which no scholar endorses at present. Prof. Oldenberg boldly rejects the Sinhalese tradition that Mahinda brought the sacred texts to Ceylon. He compares the Pāli language to that of the cave inscriptions in Mahārāshṭra and of the epigraph of king Khāravela in Hāthigumphā in Orissa, *i.e.* old Kaliṅga, says that they are essentially the same dialect and comes to the conclusion that the Ti-piṭaka was brought to the Island from the peninsula of South India, either from Mahārāshṭra or Kaliṅga, with the natural spread of Buddhism southwards [1]. I am afraid, I cannot agree with Prof. Oldenberg in his first conclusion. On the contrary, I agree with

[1] *Vinaya-Piṭakam*, Vol. I, Intro. pp. liv-lv.

Prof. Rhys Davids that the Sinhalese tradition that Buddhism was introduced into Ceylon by Mahinda is well-founded and must be accepted as true. On the other hand, Prof. Oldenberg has, I think, correctly pointed out that Pāli of Buddhist scriptures is widely divergent from Māgadhī but is essentially the same as the dialect of the old inscriptions found in Mahārāshṭra or Kaliṅga. The truth of the matter is that the Aryans, who colonised Mahārāshṭra and Kalinga [1], spoke practically the same dialect; as is evidenced by inscriptions, and that when they went still farther southwards and occupied Ceylon, they naturally introduced their own dialect there, as is also evidenced by the incriptions discovered in the Island. I have told you before that the Aryan colonisation of Ceylon was complete long prior to the advent of the Mauryas, and we must, therefore, suppose that this dialect was already being spoken when Mahinda came and introduced Buddhism. Now, we have a passage in the *Chullavagga* [2] of

[1] Personally I think, the Aryans went to Kaliṅga not by the eastern, but by the southern route. It is worthy of note that while the Pāli Buddhist canon knows Aṅga and Magadha and Assaka (Aśmaka) and Kaliṅga, it does not know Vaṅga, Puṇḍra and Suhma—exactly the countries intervening between Aṅga and Kaliṅga, through which they would certainly have passed and where they certainly would have been settled if they had gone to Kaliṅga by the eastern route. There is, therefore, nothing strange in the dialect of Kaliṅga being the same as that of Mahārāshṭra or the Pāli.

[2] V. 33. 1.

the *Vinaya-piṭaka*, in which Buddha distinctly ordains that his word was to be conveyed by different Bhikshus in their different dialects. The Māgadhī of the sacred texts brought by Mahinda must thus have been replaced by Pāli, the dialect of Ceylon, and we can perfectly understand how in this gradual replacement a few Magadhisms of the original may here and there have escaped this weeding-out, especially as Māgadhī and Pāli were not two divergent languages but only two dialects of one and the same language.

Lecture II.

POLITICAL HISTORY.

In this lecture I intend treating of the Political history of the period we have selected, *viz.* approximately from 650 to 325 B.C. No good idea of this history is possible unless we first consider the question: What were the biggest territorial divisions known at this time? The most central of these divisions is, as you are aware, the *Madhya-deśa* or the Middle Country. According to Manu [1], it denotes the land between the Himālaya in the north, the Vindhya in the south, Prayāga or Allāhābād in the east, and Vinaśana or the place where the Sarasvatī disappears, in the west. It is true that the laws of Manu were put into their present form after 200 B.C., but I have no doubt that by far the greater portion of it belongs to a much earlier period. Manu's description of the Middle Country *e.g.* appears to be older than that we find in the Buddhist Pāli canon, because the easternmost point of the Madhyadeśa was Prayāga in Manu's time, whereas that mentioned in the Buddhist works is far to the east of it. It will thus be seen that the Middle Country has not been described by Manu only but also in Buddhist

---

[1] II. 21.

scriptures. This description occurs in the Vinaya-Piṭaka[1] in connection with the Avanti-Dakshiṇāpatha country where the Buddhist monk Mahā-Kachchāyana was carrying on his missionary work. Avanti-Dakshiṇāpatha was, we are told, outside the Middle Country, and it appears that Buddhism had not made much progress there when Mahā-Kachchāyana began his work. When a new member was received into the Buddhist order, the necessary initiation ceremony had to be performed before a chapter of at least ten monks. This was the rule ordained by Buddha, but this was well-nigh impossible in the Avanti-Dakshiṇāpatha country as there were very few Bhikshus there. Mahā-Kachchāyana, therefore, sent a pupil of his to Buddha to get the rule relaxed. Buddha, of course, relaxed the rule and laid down that in all provinces outside the Middle Country a chapter of four Bhikshus was quite sufficient. It was, however, necessary to specify the boundaries of the Middle Country, and this was done by Buddha with his characteristic precision. To the east, we are told, was the town called Kajaṅgala, beyond that is Mahāsālā. To the south-east is the river Salalavatī, to the south is the town Setakaṇṇika, to the west is the Brāhmaṇ village called Thūna, and to the north is the mountain called Usīraddhaja. Unfortunately none of these boundary places here

[1] Text. I. 197; Trans, SBE. II. 38.

specified have been identified except one. This exception is the easterly point, *viz.* Kajaṅgala, which, according to Prof. Rhys Davids, must have been situated nearly 70 miles east of modern Bhāgalpur.[1] In the time of Buddha, therefore, the eastern limit of the Middle Country had extended nearly 400 miles eastward of Prayāga which was its eastern most point in Manu's time. Now there cannot be any doubt that Madhyadeśa was looked upon as a territorial division. We find constant references to it in the Buddhist Jātakas. Thus in one place we read of two merchants going from Utkala or Oṛisā to the Majjhima Deśa or Middle Country.[2] This clearly shows that Oṛisā was not included in the Middle Country. But we read of Videha being situated in it.[3] Again, we hear of hermits fearing to descend from the Himālayas to go into Majjhima Deśa, because the people there are too learned.[4] It will thus be quite clear that Majjhima Deśa or Madhya Deśa was a name not created by literary authors, but was actually in vogue among the people and denoted some particular territorial division. It was with reference to this Middle Country that the terms Dakshiṇāpatha and Uttarāpatha

---

[1] JRAS., 1904, 87-8.

[2] *Jāt.* I. 80.

[3] Ibid. III. 364.

[4] Ibid. III. 115-6.

seem to have come into use. Dakshiṇāpatha, I think, originally meant the country to the south not of the Vindhya so much as of the Madhyadeśa. This is clear from the fact that we find mention made of Avanti-Dakshiṇāpatha. I have just told you that it was in this country that the Buddhist missionary Mahā-Kachchāyana preached. It is worthy of note that Avanti was a very extensive country and that in Buddhist works we sometimes hear of Ujjenī[1] and sometimes of Māhissatī[2] as being its capital. Ujjenī is, of course, the well-known Ujjain, and Māhissatī is the same as the Sanskrit Māhishmatī and has been correctly identified with Māndhātā[3] on the Narmadā in the Central Provinces. It, therefore, seems that Ujjain was the capital of the northern division of Avanti, which was known simply as the Avanti country and Māhissatī of the southern division, which was, therefore, called Avanti-Dakshiṇāpatha. Now, Māndhātā, with which Māhissatī has been identified, is not to the south of the Vindhyas, but rather in the range itself, and as it was the capital of a country, this country must necessarily have included a portion of Central India immediately to the north of this mountain range, its southern portion having coincided with Vidarbha.

---

[1] Ibid. IV. 390.

[2] SBB. III. 270.

[3] JRAS. 1910. 445-6.

This country of Avanti-Dakshiṇāpatha was thus not exactly to the south of the Vindhya as its upper half was to the north of this range. And yet it has been called Dakshiṇāpatha.[1] And it seems to have been called Dakshiṇāpatha, because it was to the south not so much of the Vindhya as of the Middle Country. The same appears to be the case with the term Uttarāpatha. One Jātaka speaks of certain horse-dealers as having come from Uttarāpatha to Bārāṇasī or Benares.[2] Uttarāpatha cannot here signify Northern India, because Benares itself is in Northern India. Evidently it denotes a country at least outside and to the north of the Kāśi kingdom whose capital was Benares. As the horses of the dealers just referred to are called *sindhava*, it clearly indicates that they came from the banks of the Sindhu or the Indus. We have seen that according to Manu the Sarasvatī formed the western boundary of the Madhyadeśa. And the Indus is as much to the north as to the west of the Sarasvatī and therefore of Madhyadeśa. It was thus with reference to the Middle Country that the name Uttarāpatha also was devised. Up to the tenth century A.D., we find the term Uttarāpatha used in this sense.[3] Thus

---

[1] See also the name Avantī-dakkhiṇāpatha occurring in *Jāt.* III. 462. 16.

[2] II. 287. 15.

[3] In the *Divyāvadāna* (Cowell and Neil, p. 407) Takshaśilā is placed in the Uttarāpatha. But it is not clear that this Uttarāpatha excluded Madhyadeśa.

when Prabhākaravardhana, king of Sthāṇvīśvara, sent his son Rājyavardhana to invade the Hūṇa territory in the Himālayas, Bāṇa (*cir.* 625 A.D.) author of the *Harshacharita*, represents him to have gone to the Uttarāpatha.[1] As the Hūṇa territory has thus been placed in the Uttarāpatha, it is clear that Prabhākaravardhana's kingdom was excluded from it. And as Sthāṇvīśvara, capital of Prabhākaravardhana, is Ṭhānesar and is on this side of the Sarasvatī, his kingdom was understood to be included in the Madhyadeśa, with reference to which alone the Hūṇa territory seems to have been described as being in the Uttarāpatha. Similarly, the poet Rājaśekhara (880-920 A.D.), in his *Kāvya-mīmāṁsā*,[2] places Uttarāpatha on the other side of Pṛithūdaka, which, we know, is Pehoa in the Karnal District, Panjāb, *i.e.* on the western border of the Middle Country. It is, therefore, clear that the terms Dakshiṇāpatha and Uttarāpatha came into vogue only in regard to the Madhyadeśa. It must, however, be borne in mind that although Uttarāpatha in Northern India denoted the country north of the Madhyadeśa, in Southern India even in Bāṇa's time the term denoted Northern India. Thus Harshavardhana, Bāṇa's patron, has been described in South India

---

[1] *Harshacharita* (BSPS. LXVI), p. 210.

[2] (GOS.I), p. 94. l. 8.

inscriptions as *Śrīmad-Uttarāpath-ādhipati*, *i.e.* sovereign of Uttarāpatha, which must here signify North India.[3]

We thus see that the whole of the region occupied by the Aryans was at this early period divided into three parts, *viz.* Madhyadeśa, Uttarāpatha and Dakshiṇāpatha. Let us now see what the political divisions were. In no less than four places the *Aṅguttara-Nikāya* mentions what appears to be a stereotyped list of the *Soḷasa Mahā-janapada*, *i e.* the Sixteen Great Countries. This list is certainly familiar to those of you who have read Rhys Davids' *Buddhist India*. It is as follows :—

1.	Aṅgā.	9.	Kurū.
2.	Magadhā.	10.	Pañchālā.
3.	Kāsī.	11.	Machchhā.
4.	Kosalā.	12.	Sūrasenā.
5.	Vajjī.	13.	Assakā.
6.	Mallā.	14.	Avantī.
7.	Chetī.	15.	Gandhārā.
8.	Vaṁsā.	16.	Kambojā.

Now, if we look to this list, we shall find that here we have got the names not of countries proper but of peoples. It is curious that the name of a people was employed to denote the country they occupied. The custom was certainly prevalent in ancient times, but has now fallen into desuetude.

---

[3] JBBRAS., XIV. 26 ; I.A. VIII, 46.

Secondly, two of these names are not of peoples but of tribes, *viz.* the Vajjī and the Mallā. Thirdly, we seem to have here a specification, by pairs, of the conterminous countries. Aṅgā and Magadhā thus are one pair, Kāsī and Kosalā another, Kurū and Pañchālā a third, and so on, and there can be no doubt that the countries of each pair are contiguous with each other. Other points too are worth noting about this list, but they can be best understood when we come to know the more or less correct geographical position of the countries.

Let us take the first pair, *viz.* Aṅgā and Magadhā. That they were conterminous is clear *e.g.* from one Jātaka story,[1] which tells us that the citizens of Aṅga and Magadha were travelling from one land to another and staying in a house on the marches of the two *raṭṭhas*, *i.e.* kingdoms. This shows that they were not only contiguous but separate kingdoms in the 7th century B.C., the social life of which period the Jātakas are believed to depict. In the time of Buddha, Aṅga was first independent, but came afterwards to be annexed to Magadha. The river Champā separated Aṅga from Magadha.[2] On this river was the capital of Aṅga which also was called Champā and has been identified by Cunningham with Bhāgalpur.[3] One Jātaka

[1] II. 211. I & ff. [2] *Jāt.* IV. 454. 11. [3] ASR.XV. 31.

story calls it Kālachampā, and places it 60 *yojanas* from Mithilā. The capital of Magadha was Rājagṛiha, modern Rājgīr. Strictly speaking, there were two capitals here—one, the more ancient, called Girivraja because it was a veritable 'cow-pen of hills' being enclosed by the five hills of Rājgīr, and the other,[1] Rājagṛiha proper, the later town built at the foot of the hills. Shortly after the death of Buddha the capital of Magadha was transferred from Rājagṛiha to Pāṭaliputra, modern Paṭnā.

We shall take up the next pair, *viz.* Kāsī and Kosalā. Kāsi-raṭṭha was an independent kingdom before the rise of Buddhism. In the time of Buddha, however, it formed part of Kosala. The capital of Kāsi-raṭṭha was Bārāṇasī, *i.e.* Benares, so called perhaps after the great river Bārāṇasi.[2] Kāsi, it is worthy of note, was the name of a country and not of a town. Kāsipura, of course, denoted Benares, but in the sense of the capital (*pura*) of the Kāsi country. Bārāṇasī had other names also. Thus it was called Surundhana[3] in the Udaya Birth, Sudassana[4] in the Chullasutasoma Birth, Brahmavaddhana[5] in the Soṇanandana Birth, Pupphavatī[6] in the

---

[1] *Mahābhārata, Sabhā* 21. 1-3.

[2] *Index to the Jātaka* (*Jāt.* VII. 92) under *Bārāṇasi-mahānadī.*

[3] *Jāt.* IV. 104. 15, 18.

[4] Ibid. IV. 119. 28; V. 177, 12, etc.

[5] Ibid. IV. 119. 29; V. 312. 19, etc.

[6] Ibid. IV. 119. 29; VI. 131, 11, etc.

Khaṇḍahala Birth and Ramma City[1] in the Yuvañjaya Birth. Its sixth name was Molinī.[2] Kosala is called *anantara-sāmanta* to, *i.e.* immediately bordering on, Kāsi in one Jātaka. The capital of Kosala is Sāvatthi or Śrāvastī, which, we now know beyond all doubt, is Maheṭh of the village group Saheṭh-Maheṭh on the borders of the Gonda and Bahraich Districts of the United Provinces.[3] Another important town of this country was Sāketa, which was certainly the capital of Kosala in the period immediately preceding Buddha, as is clear from the Jātakas.[4] Cunningham has shown that this Sāketa can be no other than Ayodhyā, modern Oudh.[5]

The third pair we have to consider is Vajjī and Mallā. I have already told you that they are the names, not of peoples, but of tribes. The Vajjī were known also as Lichchhavis. Videha and some parts of Kosala appear to have been held by them. Their capital was Vesāli or Vaiśālī which has been identified with Basaṛh of the Muzaffarpur District of Bihār.[6]

Then comes the pair—Chetī and Vaṁsā. In the Jātakas mention has been made of Chetaraṭṭha or Chetiya-raṭṭha, and at one place we are told that its capital was

[1] Ibid. IV. 119. 26, etc.

[2] Ibid. IV. 15. 20, etc.

[3] JRAS., 1909, p. 1066 & ff.

[4] See *e.g. Jāt.* III. 270. 15.

[5] ASR. I. 320.

[6] ASI., AR., 1903-4, 82-3.

Sotthivati-nagara.[1] I have no doubt that Cheta or Chetiya is the same as the Sanskrit Chaidya or Chedi, which occurs even in the Ṛigveda[2] and corresponds roughly to the modern Bundelkhaṇḍ. The Vaṁsā are identical with the Vatsas, whose capital was Kauśāmbī. This last has been identified by Sir Alexander Cunningham with Kosam on the Jumnā, about thirty miles south of west from Allāhābād.[3]

Kuru and Pañchāla have been known to be contiguous countries since the Vedic period. The capital of the Kuru country was Indapatta or Indraprastha near Delhi, and that of Pañchāla Kāmpilya which has been identified with Kampil on the old Ganges between Budaon and Farrukhabad in U. P.[4] Both these must be Dakshiṇa-Kuru and Dakshiṇa-Pañchāla. The capital of Uttara-Pañchāla was Ahichchhatra or Ahikshetra according to the Mahābhārata. Mention of Uttara-Kuru we meet with both in the early Brahmanical and Buddhist literature, but its capital is not yet known.

As regards Machchha and Sūrasena, the former doubtless corresponds to the Sanskrit Matsya. The Matsya people and country have been known to us from early times, being mentioned as early as the Śatapatha[5] and Gopatha[6] Brāhmaṇas and the Kaushītaki Upanishad.[7]

---

[1] *Jāt.* III. 454. 19-20.

[2] VIII. 5. 37-9.

[3] ASR. I. 304-5 ; also JRAS., 1898, 503.

[4] ASR. XI. 12 ; JRAS., 1899, 313.

[5] XIII. 5. 4.9.

[6] I. 2. 9.

[7] IV. 1.

Matsya originally included parts of Alwar, Jaipur and Bharatpur, and was the kingdom of the king Virāṭa of the Mahābhārata, in whose court the five Pāṇḍava brothers resided *incognito* during the last year of their banishment.[1] His capital has been identified with Bairāṭ in the Jaipur State. The Sūrasenas occupied the country whose capital was Madhurā *i.e.* Mathurā, on the Jumnā. In Buddha's time the king of Madhurā was styled Avanti-putta, showing that on his mother's side he was connected with the royal family of Ujjain. It is worthy of note that according to Manu, the Kurukshetra, the Matsyas, the Pañchālas and the Śūrasenakas comprised *Brahmarshi-deśa* or the land of the Brāhmaṇ Ṛishis.[2]

The Assakas and the Avantis have been associated together in the Soṇa-Nanda-Jātaka.[3] The first obviously are the Aśmakas of the Bṛihat-saṁhitā.[4] In early Pāli literature, Assaka with its capital Potana or Potalī has, on the one hand, been distinguished from Muḷaka with its capital Patiṭṭhāna (Paiṭhaṇ),[5] and, on the other,

---

[1] PR., WC.. 1909-10, 44.

[2] II. 19.

[3] *Jāt.*, V. 317. 24.

[4] IA., XXII. 174.

[5] In the *Sutta-Nipāta* (V. 977) the Assaka (Aśmaka) country has been associated with Muḷaka with its capital Patiṭṭhāna and mentioned as situated immediately to the south of the latter but along the river Godāvarī (Vs. 977 & 1010-1). See also p. 4 and n. 3 supra.

from Kaliṅga with its capital Dantapura.[1] But as Assaka is here contrasted with Avanti, it seems to have included Muḷaka and also perhaps Kaliṅga.[2] Avanti also here includes the two well-known divisions referred to above—the northern division called simply Avanti country with its capital Ujjain and the southern Avanti-Dakshiṇāpatha with its capital Māhissatī.

The last pair is Gandhāra and Kamboja. The former included West Panjāb and East Afghānistān. Its capital was Takkasilā or Takshaśilā,[3] whose ruins are spread near Sarāī-Kālā in the Rāwalpiṇḍī District, Panjāb. It is very difficult to locate Kamboja. According to one view they were a Northern Himālayan people, and according to another the Tibetans. But in our period they were probably settled to the north-west of the Indus and are the same

---

[1] *Jāt.* III. 3. 3-4.

[2] Assaka is similarly contrasted with Avanti in *Jāt.* V, 317. 24. In the Dīgha-Nikāya, Kaliṅga, Assaka, and Avanti are contradistinguished (SBB. III. 270) where Assaka must have comprised Muḷaka.

[3] *Jāt.*, I. 191. II; II. 47. 11, etc., etc. In the Mahābhārata two capitals of Gandhāra are mentioned, *viz.* Takshaśilā and Pushkarāvatī, the former situated to the east and the latter to the west of the Indus. In Aśoka's time Takshaśilā does not appear to have been the capital of Gandhāra, for from his Rock Edict XIII we see that Gandhāra was not in his dominions proper but was feudatory to him. On the other hand, from Separate Orissa Edict I we learn that Takshaśilā, was under him as one of his sons was stationed there. Evidently Takshaśilā was not the capital of Gandhāra in Aśoka's time. This agrees with the statement of Ptolemy that the Gandarai (Gandhāra) country was to the west of the Indus with its city Proklais *i.e.* (Pushkarāvatī) (IA. XIII. 348-49).

as Kambujiya of the old Persian inscriptions. Their capital is not known.

It will be seen that the different political divisions, mentioned in the above list, were in existence shortly before the time of Buddha. We know that during his lifetime Aṅga ceased to be an independent kingdom, and was annexed to Magadha, and that the territory of Kāsi was incorporated into the Kosala dominions. If we, however, turn to the Jātakas, we find that both Aṅga and Kāsi were independent countries. The Champeyya-Jātaka [1] *e g.* speaks of Aṅga and Magadha as two distinct kingdoms, whose rulers were constantly at war with each other. Kāsi and Kosala are similarly represented in the Mahāsīlava-Jātaka and Asātarūpa-Jātaka [2] as being two independent countries and their kings fighting with each other. The political divisions enumerated in the Aṅguttara-Nikāya were, therefore, existing prior, but only just prior, to the time when Buddha flourished, because we have the mention of the Vajjī and Mallā in this list. It is worthy of note that they are mentioned in the Jātakas but only in the introductions to them and never in the stories themselves.

Evidently, therefore, these tribes came to be known after the period represented by the Jātakas but before that of the origin of Buddhism. It will

---

[1] *Jāt.* IV. 454 & ff.

[2] Ibid., I. 262 & ff and 409 & ff.

thus be observed that early in the sixth century B.C., India, *i.e.* that portion of India which was colonised by the Aryans at that time, was split up into a number of tiny States, living independently and sometimes fighting with one another. There was no supreme ruler to whom they owed fealty. The Purāṇas tell the same tale. They distinctly state that along with the rulers of Magadha flourished other dynasties, such as Aikshvākavas or kings of Kosala, Pañchālas, Kāseyas, Aśmakas, Kurus, Maithilas and so forth.[1] This clearly shows that about 600 B.C., India occupied by the Aryans was divided into several small kingdoms and that there was no imperial dynasty to which the others were subordinate. The most important of these tiny dynasties is that of Brahmadatta reigning at Bārāṇasī and ruling over Kāsiraṭṭha. The family also seems to have been called Brahmadatta after this king. Thus in the Jātakas every prince who was heir-apparent to the throne of Bārāṇasī has been styled Brahmadatta-kumāra. In the Matsya-Purāṇa[2] also, a dynasty consisting of one hundred Brahmadattas has been referred to. In the Jātakas no less than six kings of Bārāṇasī have been mentioned besides Brahmadatta. They are Uggasena,

---

[1] Pargiter, 23-4.

[2] (ASS. Ed.), p. 556, V. 72; I am indebted for this reference to Mr. Harit Krishna Deb.

Dhanañjaya, Mahāsīlava, Saṁyama, Vissasena and Udayabhadda.[1] In the Purāṇas Brahmadatta is represented to have been followed in succession by Yogasena, Vishvaksena, Udaksena and Bhallāṭa.[2] There can be no doubt that Vishvaksena and Udaksena of the Purāṇas are the same as Vissasena and Udayabhadda of the Jātakas. Bhallāṭa of the Purāṇas, again, is most probably Bhallāṭiya of the Bhallāṭiya-Jātaka.[3]

When Buddha lived and preached, there were four kingdoms, *viz.* Magadha, Kosala, Vatsa and Avanti. The most prominent of these was Magadha, whose rulers, as we shall see subsequently, rose to the position of paramount sovereigns. From Pāli Buddhist canon which pertains to a period only slightly later than the demise of Buddha and which consequently is trustworthy, we learn that Chaṇḍa-Pradyota of Avanti, Udayana of Vatsa territory, Pasenadi and his son Viḍūḍabha of Kosala, and Bimbisāra and his son Ajātaśatru of Magadha were contemporaries of Buddha. The kings were thus contemporaries of one another. This point is worth grasping as this synchronism is the only sheet-anchor in the troubled sea of chronology

---

[1] *Jāt.*. IV. 458. 13; III. 97. 23; I. 262. 8; V. 354. 9; II. 345. 19; IV. 104. 22 & 25.

[2] *Vāyu-P.* (ASS. Ed.), p. 376, VS. 180-2; *Vishṇu-P.*, pt. IV cap. 19.

[3] *Jāt.* IV. 437. 16.

in the period we have selected. The only chronicle that is relied on for this period is the Purāṇas, but it is a hopeless task to reduce the chaos of the Purāṇic accounts to any order. Some attempts [1] no doubt have recently been made to deduce a consistent political history from these materials, but without any success so far as I can see.

I have just informed you that in the time of Buddha there were four important kingdoms, flourishing side by side. They were also connected by matrimonial alliances as might naturally be expected. For our description we shall first take Udayana of Kausāmbī, and Pradyota, ruler of Ujjain. A long account of Udayana is contained in the *Kathā-sarit-sāgara*, but the greater portion of it, I am afraid, is untrustworthy. According to the Purāṇas he pertained to the Paurava dynasty.[2] The same authority tells us that his father's name was Śatānīka. Bhāsa, the earliest Sanskrit dramatist that we know at present, has composed two dramas describing incidents from Udayana's life, *viz. Svapna-Vāsavadattā* and *Pratijñā-Yaugandharāyaṇa*. From these it appears that he was the son of Śatānīka and grandson of Sahasrānīka and

---

[1] Mr. S. V. Venkateswara Ayyar's *The Ancient History of Magadha* (IA., xlv. 8-16 & 28-31); Mr. K. P. Jayaswal's *The Śaiśunāka and Maurya Chronology etc.* (JBORS., 1915, 67 & ff.)

[2] Pargiter, pp. 7 & 66.

belonged to the Bhārata family.[1] As he is called Vaidehīputra, his mother appears to have been daughter of the king of Videha. Udayana's first Queen was Vāsavadattā, daughter of the king of Ujjain, who is called Pradyota Mahāsena by Bhāsa but Chaṇḍa Pradyota in Buddhist works. According to the Buddhist tradition, Udayana had two more queens, *viz.* Sāmavatī and Māgandiyā. The latter was his crowned queen and was daughter of a Brāhmaṇ. According to the Brāhmaṇic accounts he had two queens only, *viz.* Vāsavadattā and Padmāvatī. His second queen, Padmāvatī, was sister to Darśaka, king of Rājagṛiha, Magadha. Scholars of the saner type have assigned Bhāsa to the third century A.D., and Bhāsa apparently followed the tradition which was current in his time. He does not, however, seem to be correct in accepting the tradition which makes Padmāvatī, sister to Darśaka, as will be shown shortly when we come to treat of the Magadha dynastics. Udayana had a lute called Ghoshavatī,[2] whose sound captivated the elephants and by means of which he captured them. He had a she-elephant named Bhaddavatikā, to which he owed his life, queen and kingdom.[3]

---

[1] Bhāsa speaks of this family as *prākaśa-rājarshi-nāmadheyo* and *Ved-ākshara-samavāya-pravishṭo* (*Pratijñā-Y.*, p. 34).

[2] This seems to have been an heir-loom of the Bhārata family to which Udayana belonged and which was noted for proficiency in music (*Pratijñā-Y.*, pp. 34-5).

[3] *Jāt.* III. 384.

The two dramas of Bhāsa referred to above supply us with many interesting items of information which, when they are brought to a focus, throw a flood of light upon the political condition of the period. The king, that seems to have been dreaded most when Buddha lived, was not Ajātaśatru, Pasenadi or Udayana, but Pradyota who is known both as Mahāsena or "possessed of a large army"[1] and Chaṇḍa or "terrible."[2] We know from the *Majjhima-Nikāya* that even such a powerful king as Ajātaśatru was thrown on his defensive and was engaged on fortifying his capital Rājagṛiha when Pradyota invaded his territory, instead of meeting him openly in battle. Before, however, he attacked Magadha, he thought of subjugating the neighbouring province of Vatsa. But he was afraid of the undaunted bravery of Udayana and the political sagacity of his prime-minister Yaugandharāyaṇa. He, therefore, resorted to a ruse. He knew of the inordinate fondness of Udayana for capturing wild elephants with the captivating sounds of his *vīṇā*. An artificial elephant was set up in the jungles of the Narmadā just where the boundaries of the Avanti and Vatsa kingdoms

---

[1] Vāsavadattā herself says that her father was called Mahāsena on account of his large army (*tasya bala-parimāṇa-nirvṛittaṁ nāmadheyaṁ Mahāsena iti*—*Svapna-V.*, 20.).

[2] In the same drama Udayana speaks of Pradyota as *prithivyāṁ rāja-vaṁśyānām=uday-āsta-maya-prabhuḥ* (p. 67).

met, and in the body of the elephant were concealed a number of select warriors. Udayana fell a victim to this trap, put up a heroic fight to free himself, but was taken prisoner and carried away to Ujjain, where however, he was accorded chivalrous treatment by Mahāsena. When Yaugandharāyaṇa learnt that his master had fallen into the hands of a neighbouring king, he hastened to his release. He turned a Buddhist monk along with another minister and stole into Ujjain. He found that the release of Udayana had become a complicated affair by the latter having fallen in love with Vāsavadattā, Mahāsena's daughter. He, however, devised a way out of this difficulty. One of his men was made a Mahaut of Vāsavadattā, and on an appointed day the two lovers managed to elope, leaving Yaugandharāyaṇa and his fighting band to cover their flight. At first, Mahāsena was furious, but he soon relented, and in the absence of the lovers themselves the proper marriage ceremonies were performed over their portraits.

Kauṭilya in his Arthaśāstra [1] says that when it is impossible to ward off danger from all sides, a king should run away, leaving all that belongs to him; for, if he lives, his return to power is certain as was the case with Suyātra and Udayana. We know from the *Svapna-*

[1] p. 358.

Vāsavadattā that Udayana had to flee from his kingdom to a frontier village called Lāvāṇaka. The enemy, who overran his territory, was Āruṇi,[1] who appears to have been ruling to the north of the Ganges. Might he be a king of Kosala? At any rate, the *Ratnāvalī* clearly represents a king of Kosala to be Udayana's enemy. The disaster was thought by Yaugandharāyaṇa to be so serious that the help of Pradyota, which was naturally expected, was not regarded to be sufficient, and marriage alliance with the Royal House of Magadha considered indispensable. But this was possible only if Udayana agreed to marry Padmāvatī, sister of the Magadha king. Udayana, however, was so attached to Vāsavadattā that he could not brook the idea of having another wife so long as she was alive. Vāsavadattā must, therefore, disappear for a time, thought the Prime-minister, so that Udayana could believe her to be dead and could therefore agree to marry Padmāvatī. When once the king was out a-hunting, the place was set on fire, as previously planned, after Vāsavadattā and Yaugandharāyaṇa quietly left it. Everybody thought that the latter two had been consigned to the flames. On his return when the king knew about the disaster, he was overwhelmed with grief, from which, however, in course of

[1] pp. 60-1

time he recovered. There was thus no difficulty in bringing about the contemplated marriage alliance, and Udayana was married to Padmāvatī. Soon after his marriage and before he left Rājagṛiha, his minister Rumaṇvat had already apparently with the help sent by Mahāsena [1] driven away Aruṇi from the Vatsa kingdom and to the north of the Ganges, where it seems he was joined by Udayana along with the forces of the Magadha king, with the express object of killing Āruṇi. And we may assume that he soon succeeded in accomplishing his object.

According to the Pāli Buddhist canon, Udayana had a son named Bodhi, who most probably is identical with Vahīnara of the Purāṇas. Bodhi is represented as ruling over the Bhagga country at Suṁsumāragiri, apparently as Yuvarāja. [2] He got a *vaḍḍhaki* or carpenter to build for him a palace which he called Kokanada, but fearing that the artisan may build a similar excellent palace for another prince, Bodhi had his eyes plucked out. There is a *suttanta* in the *Majjhima-Nikāya* which is devoted to him and is called Bodhi-rāja-kumāra-sutta. Beyond this we know nothing reliable about this dynasty. [3]

---

[1] There can be no doubt that Mahāsena sent succour to Udayana as the latter acknowledges it (*Svapna V.*, p. 68).

[2] *Jāt.* III. 157.

[3] For the anecdote about Udayana and Piṇḍola, see *Jāt.* IV. 375.

Such is also the case with the dynasty that ruled over the Avanti country with its capital at Ujjain. I have just mentioned that a king of this family was Pradyota, who was a contemporary of Buddha. The Purāṇas make him the founder of the dynasty. In Bhāsa's dramas he is frequently called Mahāṣena. From his queen Aṅgāravatī he had a daughter Vāsavadattā espoused by Udayana, as mentioned above. We do not know much about his conquests, and all we know about him in this respect is the statement of the *Majjhima-Nikāya*[1] that Ajātaśatru, king of Magadha, was fortifying his capital Rājagṛiha because he was afraid of an invasion of his territory by Pradyota. Bhāsa speaks of his two sons, *viz.* Gopāla and Pālaka.[2] Gopāla, it is said, was of the same age as Udayana. *Kathā-sarit-sāgara*[3] says that after the death of Pradyota, Gopāla abdicated the throne of Ujjain in favour of his younger brother Pālaka. This is not improbable, and also accounts for the omission of his name in the Purāṇas. The *Mṛichchhakaṭika*[4] further tells us that Pālaka was ousted by Āryaka, son of Gopāla, who was in hiding for a long time in a settlement of herdsmen. What appears to be the truth is that Pradyota was succeeded not by Gopāla

[1] III. 7.

[2] *Pratijñā-Y.*, 35.

[3] III. 62-3. I am indebted to Mr. H. K. Deb for this reference.

[4] (BSS. Ed.) pp. 189 & 306.

but by his younger brother Pālaka, and that Gopāla's son Āryaka, not liking the idea of being deprived of the throne, conspired against his uncle, and succeeded in usurping the throne. The Purāṇas omit the name of Gopāla,—which is not strange as he resigned the throne in favour of his brother, and mention those of Pālaka and Āryaka. The latter is mentioned as Ajaka, which I have no doubt stands for Ajjaka *i.e.* Aryaka.[1] They, however, place one Viśākhayūpa between Pālaka and Āryaka—which is a mistake. Viśākhayūpa, if there was a prince of such a name in this dynasty, must have come after Āryaka. We now pass on to the Kosala dynasty. The only princes of this royal family known to us from the Buddhist works are Pasenadi and his son Viḍūḍabha. I suspect that they belonged to the Ikshvāku family described by the Purāṇas, which, in the enumeration of its members, mention one Prasenajit which, I think, is the Sanskrit form of Pasenadi. Kshudraka is mentioned as the name of Prasenajit's son, and it is possible that this was another name of Viḍūḍabha. *Majjhima-Nikāya*[2] calls Pasenadi King of Kāsi-Kosala, and from the preamble of Bhadda-sāla Jātaka,[3] we learn that the territory held by the Śākyas was also

[1] This identification was first proposed by Mr. K. P. Jayaswal (JBORS., 1915, 107).

[2] II. 111.

[3] *Jāt.*, IV. 144 & ff

subordinate to him. Pasenadi had an *amātya* called Siri-Vaḍḍha and a favourite elephant named Eka-puṇḍarīka.[1] One of his queens was Mallikā, who was originally daughter of the chief of garland-makers in Śrāvastī[2]. She was only sixteen when Pasenadi married her, and as she was married when he was at war with Ajātaśatru, she seems to have been married at his practically old age by Pasenadi. Nevertheless Mallikā predeceased him. Pasenadi had a daughter called Vajirā or Vajirī. She was married to Ajātaśatru, as I shall tell you later on. With a pious desire to become a kinsman of Buddha, Pasenadi sent envoys to the Śākyas with a request to give him a Śākya girl in marriage. The Śākyas, through their pride of birth, were unwilling to give him any girl of pure blood, and sent one Vāsabha-Khattiyā, born to a Śākya named Mahānāman from a slave woman. She was married to king Pasenadi and raised to the rank of the Chief Queen.[3] She gave birth to Viḍūḍabha, who succeeded him. When Viḍūḍabha became a grown-up boy, he went to the Śākya country against the wishes of his mother, where he was subjected to a series of indignities. There the real origin of his mother became known. The

---

[1] *Maj-N.*, II. 112.
[2] *Jāt.*, III. 405.
[3] *Aṅg.-N.*, III. 57.

news reached the ears of Pasenadi, who was enraged with the Śākyas and degraded both Vāsabha-Khattiyā and Viḍūḍabha, but reinstated them upon the intercession of Buddha. As soon as Viḍūḍabha came to the throne, he marched to the Śākya territory, massacred the Śākyas, and thus wreaked his vengeance for which he was burning ever since he came to know about the fraud practised by them. It is said that thrice Buddha dissuaded Viḍūḍabha from carrying out this wholesale carnage of the Śākyas, but it is difficult to say how far this is true. From Buddhist works we gather a great deal about the fights between the rulers of Kosala and Magadha, but about these we shall come to know shortly.

We now come to describe the dynasty or rather the dynasties that ruled over Magadha. The first of these is the family to which belonged Bimbisāra and his son Ajātaśatru, who, you will remember, were contemporaries of Buddha. The authority which is generally followed in giving an account of this family is the Purāṇas. But there is another authority, which is more reliable, but which is neglected. I mean the Sinhalese chronicle Mahāvaṁsa. The Purāṇic account, I am afraid, is anything but satisfactory, so far as the order of succession, at any rate, is concerned, though I quite believe the scraps of information they supply in regard to some princes. According to the Purāṇas Śiśunāga was the founder of this dynasty and Bimbisāra was its fourth prince. And they also tell us that the Pradyota dynasty consisted of five kings and that they were supplanted by Śiśunāga. Bimbisāra is thus ten generations removed from Pradyota, whereas, as a matter of fact, we know that both were contemporaries of each other, being contemporaries of Buddha. Again, though the tradition as to individual names is not very unstable in the different Purāṇas, the same cannot be said in regard to the period of the individual reigns which vary considerably. What is also strange is that they assign a period of 363 years to ten consecutive reigns, *i.e.* at least 36 years to each reign which is quite preposterous and utterly unknown to Indian History.[1] This indicates a desperate attempt on the part of the Purāṇas to fill up the gaps in the chronology anyhow—an inference which entirely agrees with their attempt at reduplicating names and assigning them to consecutive kings, such as Kshemadharman and Kshemavit, Nandivardhana, and Mahānandin, and so fourth. Further, it is worthy of note that the Mahāvaṁsa mentions het name of the king Muṇḍa, which is entirely omitted from the Purāṇa list. The existence

[1] Most of these arguments have been already urged by W. Geiger in his translation of the *Mahāvaṁsa* (PTS. Ed.), Intro. xliv & ff.

of this king is now sufficiently attested by the *Anguttara-Nikāya* and the *Aśokāvadāna*. Next, the Mahāvaṁsa makes Udayabhadda (or Udāyi) the immediate successor of Ajātaśatru, but the Purāṇas place one Darśaka in between. That surely is highly questionable, because the Dīgha-Nikāya speaks of Udayabhadra as Ajātaśatru's son, but we have no such evidence in respect of Darśaka. I am aware, it may be argued, that Darśaka has, as a matter of fact, been mentioned by Bhāsa in the *Svapna-Vāsavadattā*, as a king of Magadha whose sister Padmāvatī was married to Udayana of Kauśāmbī, and that it is possible that he was another son of Ajātaśatru and might have been the latter's immediate successor, his brother Udayabhadra coming to the throne after him. But this argument does not appear to be sound to me, because how old, I ask, could Udayana be when he married Padmāvatī? To make the case favourable to the other side, we will suppose that he was wedded to her in the very first year of Darśaka's accession to the throne. We know that Buddha preached not only to Udayana but also to his son Bodhi. To make the case more favourable, we shall suppose that Bodhi was then only sixteen years old, and that Bodhi was born when Udayana also was sixteen. Udayana thus must have been at least thirty-two years old, when Buddha preached to Bodhi. We will also concede that Buddha died the same year that he delivered the sermon to Bodhi. And we know that Buddha died in the eighth regnal year of Ajātaśatru and that the latter reigned twenty-four years after Buddha's death. We thus see that Udayana was at least thirty two years old when Buddha died and therefore fifty-six years old when Ajātaśatru ceased to reign. Udayana was thus married in his fifty-seventh year, *i.e.* in the first year of Darśaka's reign. Is it the proper age for the hero to make love to the heroine, and is it proper for the poet to describe it?[1] Verily there must be some mistake somewhere. Bhāsa evidently followed the tradition that was current in his time, *i.e.* most probably in the third century A. D. By that time the Purāṇas, through the corruption of their texts,

---

[1] I admit that Udayana's marriage with Padmāvatī was of a political character, and that it is quite possible to argue that it does not matter if the hero represented is in his decline of age. On the other hand, however, we have to note first that *Svapna-Vāsavadattā* is not a political drama like Mudrā-Rākshasa. Secondly, what I cannot understand is the love-sickness of the newly wedded couple which is certainly described in the drama and which such a dramatist of fine delicate sentiment as Bhāsa would certainly have suppressed if he had thought that Udayana was on the other side of fifty. On p. 35 Udayana speaks of himself as being pierced by the sixth arrow of the God of love. On p. 49 Vidūshaka refers to the *Madan-āgni-dāha* of Udayana caused by his second marriage and intensified by the bereavement of his first queen. In Act. V we are told that Padmāvatī is laid up with a headache, of course, caused through love-sickness, to remove which her meeting with Udayana is being arranged for. I am sure that all these references to the love-sickness of the lovers Bhāsa would have studiously avoided if according to him they had been an ill-assorted couple.

must have become full of contradictions and discrepancies, and must have been more than once tampered with to make them yield an intelligent story. For these reasons I cannot help thinking that it is not safe to rely upon the account furnished by the Purāṇas for this early period so far at any rate as the order of succession and the duration of individual reigns are concerned. The tradition preserved in the Mahāvaṁsa about the Magadha dynasties seems to me more reliable. At any rate, no inaccuracies or blunders have yet been detected in the account of this chronicle, which wonderfully agrees with the scraps of information which the Purāṇas furnish for some princes.

I have already told you that the two rulers of Magadha who were contemporaries of Buddha were Bimbisāra and his son Ajātaśatru. The name of the family to which Bimbisāra belonged is not definitely known, but it seems that it was Nāga. The last prince of Bimbisāra's dynasty is called Nāga-Dāsaka by the Mahāvaṁsa. The second component of the name, *viz.* Dāsaka, doubtless corresponds to the Darśaka of the Purāṇas. And the name Nāga has been prefixed to Dāsaka to distinguish him from his successor who belonged to a somewhat different family and who has therefore been called Susu-Nāga, or Little Nāga. Darśaka, and thus Bimbisāra, belonged to the Great Nāga dynasty. We do not know whether any kings of his dynasty preceded Bimbisāra. They have certainly not been mentioned by the Mahāvaṁsa, but there was no need for this chronicle to mention them, its sole object being to describe the events of the period beginning with Buddha and not anterior to him. The Purāṇas no doubt represent at least four kings to have ruled before Bimbisāra, but their authority for this period, as I have just stated, is disputable. The probability is that Bimbisāra was the founder of his dynasty, because Bimbisāra has in the Pāli Canon been called *Seniya*, which is the same thing as *Senāpati*. We know that Pushpamitra, founder of the Śuṅga dynasty, was designated *Senāpati*, and we have the authority of the Purāṇas that Pushpamitra was actually the commander-in-chief of the last king of the Maurya family that he supplanted. It is not at all impossible that Bimbisāra was the general of the Power that ruled over Magadha before him and that if he did not actually destroy it, he at any rate declared his independence and carved out a kingdom for himself. The question here arises: who could be exercising sway over Magadha prior to Bimbisāra? A passage in one of the oldest Buddhist documents speaks of Vesāli as *Māgadhaṁ puraṁ*,[1] capital of the Magadha country.

[1] *Sutta-Nipāta*, p. 185, v. 38.

If Vesāli was thus the capital of the Magadha kingdom, it is quite possible that it was at the expense of the Vajjīs that Bimbisāra secured territory for himself. According to the Purāṇas Magadha was originally held by the Bārhadratha family. Then, it seems, occurred the inroads of the Vajjīs, who held Magadha. In the early years of Buddha, Bimbisāra thus appears to have seized Magadha after expelling the Vajjīs beyond the Ganges and to have established himself at Rājagṛiha, the old capital of the kingdom. This was not the only conquest achieved by him. Bimbisāra conquered Aṅga also and incorporated it into his dominions. In the *Majjhima-Nikāya*[1] we have mention of a king of Aṅga who gave a daily pension of 500 kārshāpaṇas to a Brāhmaṇ. The name of this king has not been specified, but there can be little doubt that is was this prince from whom Bimbisāra wrested Aṅga. It was doubtless these conquests that gave Bimbisāra sovereignty over 80,000 townships,[2] the overseers of which, it appears, he was in the habit of calling to an assembly for personally discussing state matters and receiving his instructions.

The *Mahāvagga*[3] says that Bimbisāra had 500 wives. Of these one was, we know, a Vaidehī princess. According to an early Jaina

[1] II. 163. [2] *Mahāvagga*, v. 1. 1 & ff.

[3] VIII. 1. 15.

authority she was Chellanā, daughter of Cheṭaka, a Lichchavi, Chief of Vaiśālī.[1] It is quite possible that this matrimonial alliance was a result of the peace concluded after the war between Bimbisāra and the Lichchhavis. His another queen was Kosaladevī, daughter of Mahākosala, who was father of Pasenadi. The father, when he married his daughter to the king Bimbisāra, gave a village of the Kāsi country, yielding a revenue of a hundred thousand, as her *nahāna-chuṇṇa-mūla*, *i.e.* bath and perfume money.[2] From his Vaidehī queen Bimbisāra had a son called Ajātaśatru.[3] He had also another son, named Abhaya, but we do not know who the latter's mother was. When Abhaya was once going to attend upon his father, king Bimbisāra, he saw an infant exposed on a dust-heap.[4] He took up the infant, nourished him, and named him Jīvaka Komārabhachcha. Jīvaka went to Takshaśilā, and learnt the science of medicine. He returned to Rājagṛiha and showed his expert knowledge by speedily curing king Bimbisāra of fistula. Bimbisāra was so pleased that he appointed Jīvaka as physician to the royal household

[1] SBE. XXII. Intro. xiii.

[2] *Jāt.* II. 403. 15.

[3] Ibid. III. 121-2 make Kosaladevī to be Ajātaśatru's mother, and *Saṁ-N.* I. 84 speaks of him as *bhāgineyya* to Pasenadi. But this is a mistake, because in the Chullavagga Ajātaśatru is invariably called *Vedehiputto*.

[4] *Mahāvagga*, viii, 1, 4 & ff.

and to the fraternity of the Bhikshus headed by Buddha. Bimbisāra had at least two more sons. One of them was Sīlavat born at Rājagṛiha.[1] The other was Vimala-Koṇḍañña from Queen Ambapālī.[2] As Vimala bears the Brāhmaṇ clan-name of Koṇḍañña (=Kauṇḍiṇya), it appears that his mother was a Brāhmaṇ woman. The princes, Abhaya, Sīlavat and Vimala, all became Buddhist monks, probably through fear of Ajātaśatru after he became king. When by murdering his father, as we shall just see, Ajātaśatru seized the throne he must have attempted to assassinate his brothers also, who therefore must have thought it discreet to embrace Buddhism and become monks. We have got evidence at least in the case of Sīlavat whom according to the *Thera-therī-gāthā* Ajātaśatru was anxious to put to death.

I have just referred to the murder of Bimbisāra by his son Ajātaśatru. The story is just this. Being instigated by Devadatta, cousin but enemy to Buddha, Ajātaśatru conceived the design of killing his father and obtaining the kingdom. With that object in view he once entered the private chamber of the king at an unusual hour with a dagger in his hand. He was, however, seized upon by the officers in attendance and taken before the king.

---

[1] *Thera-gāthā* (trans.), 269.

[2] Ibid., 65.

On learning that his son wanted to kill him because he wanted the kingdom, Bimbisāra at once handed over the reins of government to him.[1] But the prince was not satisfied with this, and in order to make his position quite secure, he at the advice of Devadatta managed to kill his father by starvation. While once he was listening to a sermon of Buddha he was suddenly striken with remorse and confessed his sin before him[2]. Although there is no sound reason to distrust the story of this parricide, the explanation which Buddhist texts give of his name, *viz.* Ajātaśatru, scarcely deserves any credence. It is said that even when he was in his mother's womb, he conceived a longing for his father's blood, which was gratified only by the mother drinking it from the right knee of Bimbisāra, and that because he had thus been his father's enemy (*śatru*), while yet unborn (*ajāta*), he was named Ajātaśatru. This is nothing but a pun.[3]

I have told you that when king Mahākosala, father of Pasenadi, married his daughter to Bimbisāra, he granted a Kāsi village as dowry. When Ajātaśatru put Bimbisāra to death, Kosaladevī died of grief. For sometime after this queen's death, Ajātaśatru continued to enjoy the revenues of this village, but Pasenadi

---

1. *Chullavagga*, vii. 3. 5.
2. *Jāt.*, v. 261-2, *Dīgha-N.* I. 85 ; SBB., II. 94.
3. *Jāt.* III, 121-2.

resolved that no parricide should have a village which was his by right of inheritance and so confiscated it. There was thus war betwixt Ajātaśatru and Pasenadi. The former was fierce and strong, and the latter old and feeble. So Pasenadi was beaten again and again. Now, at the time when he had returned to his capital Śrāvastī after suffering his last reverse, Buddha was staying close by with his fraternity of *bhikshus*. Amongst those there were many who formerly were officers of the king. Two of these at dawn one day were discussing the nature of the war, and one of them emphatically declared that if Pasenadi but gave Ajātaśatru battle by arranging his army in the *śakaṭa-vyūha* array, he could have him like a fish in lobster pot. The king's couriers, who happened to overhear the conversation, informed him. Pasenadi seized the hint, and immediately set out with a great host. He took Ajātaśatru prisoner and bound him in chains. After a few days he released him, gave him his daughter, Princess Vajirā, in marriage, and dismissed her with that Kāsi village for her bath-money, which was for long the bone of contention between the two royal families. [1]

Ajātaśatru was at war also with the Lichchhavis of Vesāli. I have already told you that his mother was a Vaidehī Princess. This means

[1] *Jāt.* II. 237 & 403-4; IV. 343; *Saṁ.N.* I. 83-5.

that she belonged to the Lichchhavi clan. Ajātaśatru was thus at war with his relations on his mother's side. He seems to have pursued the policy inaugurated by his father. We have seen that it was at the expense of the Lichchhavis that Bimbisāra made himself master of the Magadha kingdom. And now his son Ajātaśatru conceived the design of destroying the independence of the Lichchhavis. It appears that at this time the Ganges separated the Magadha from the Videha kingdom, and that Pāṭaligrāma, which afterwards rose to great importance and became celebrated as Pāṭaliputra, was then on the frontier of the Magadha territory. At any rate, this is the impression produced on our mind on reading the *Mahāparinibbāna-sutta*,[1] which is concerned with the decease of Buddha. The same *Sutta* also gives us the impression that Pāṭaligrāma was on the road from Vesāli to Rājagṛiha. It was, therefore, absolutely necessary to fortify Pāṭaligrāma. And when, shortly before his death, Buddha visited Pāṭaligrāma, Sunīdha and Vassakāra, Chief Ministers of Magadha, were busy building a fortress there to repel the Vajjīs, *i.e.* Lichchhavis. The Jaina *Nirayāvali-sūtra* informs us that Ajātaśatru fixed a quarrel on Cheṭaka, a Lichchhavi Chief of Vesāli, his grandfather and

---

[1] I. 26; *Mahāvagga*, vi. 28. 7 & ff.

went forth to attack him.[1] Nine confederate Lichchhavi and nine confederate Malla kings came to his assistance but it was of no avail, and the Vajjīs or Lichchhavis were ere long subjected to the sway of Ajātaśatru along with the Mallas.

Ajātaśatru was succeeded by his son Udayabhadra who is no doubt the same as the Udāyin of the Purāṇas. According to the *Dīgha-Nikāya*, as we have seen, Ajātaśatru looked upon him as his favourite son, but it was this favourite son who for the sake of kingdom murdered his father, as the Mahāvaṁsa[2] tells us. The Purāṇas say that he made Kusumapura on the southern bank of the Ganges his capital.[3] Kusumapura is but another name for Pāṭaliputra, and there is nothing strange in Udayabhadra's removing his capital from Rājagṛiha to Pāṭaliputra. The Magadha kingdom was very much extended during the reign of Ajātaśatru. The dominions of the Lichchhavis and Mallas and some parts of even Kosala were annexed to it. Such an extensive kingdom required a central capital, and this idea was well fulfilled by Pāṭaliputra, which, though in the first instance it was fortified to repel and subdue the Lichchhavis, admirably served the purpose of a central seat of government.

---

[1] SBE. xxii. Intro. xiv.

[2] IV. 1.

[3] Pargiter, 22 & 69.

Udayabhadra reigned for sixteen years. He was succeeded by Anuruddha, and the latter by Muṇḍa. A period of eight years has been assigned to them. No reference to Anuruddha has so far been traceable in the Buddhist literature, but the *Aṅguttara-Nikāya*[1] does make mention of Muṇḍa, king of Pāṭaliputra. His queen, Bhadrā-devī died, and the king was simply overwhelmed with grief. His Treasurer Priyaka became intensely anxious on his account, and arranged for an interview between the king and Nārada, a Buddhist monk, who had at that time come to Pāṭaliputra in the course of his religious tour. Nārada's religious discourse made a deep impression on Muṇḍa and gave him strength of mind to overcome his grief.

Muṇḍa was succeeded by Nāga-Dāsaka. I told you a short while ago that Dāsaka of this composite name corresponded to the Darśaka of the Purāṇas, and Nāga was prefixed to his name to show that he pertained to the principal Nāga dynasty. The tradition mentioned by Bhāsa that Padmāvatī married to Udayana was his sister does not appear to be probable, and you have already seen the reasons I have set forth. The Mahāvaṁsa says that from Ajātaśatru down to Darśaka we had kings who were parricides, and that the people, who were, therefore, disgusted with this

---

[1] III. 57 & ff.

dynasty, aided one Susu-Nāga, who was an *amātya* or minister apparently of Darśaka, to oust him and secure the throne. Susu-Nāga, as I have said, does not seem to be a proper name. It denotes a branch of the Nāga family, and as sometimes a king is designated by his family name alone without specification of his individual name, the family name Susu-Nāga, or Śiśu-Nāga of the Purāṇas, has been employed to denote the usurper of Darśaka's sovereignty. Anyhow this usurper was not an outsider, but a prince of the Nāga dynasty though of a branch line. The Purāṇas inform us that Susu-Nāga annihilated the renown of the Pradyota dynasty, placed his son in Vārāṇasī or Benares, and made Girivraja (Rājgīr) his capital.[1] The Purāṇas evidently tell us that Susu-Nāga made himself master not only of Magadha but also of Avanti and Kāśi-Kosala. This seems to be correct, and to this we may add that he probably annexed the Vatsa kingdom also to his empire. We know that Pradyota, Pasenadi (Prasenajit), Bimbisāra and Udayana were contemporaries, and their families, curiously enough, became extinct four generations after them, *i. e.* about the rise of Susu-Nāga. The latter was thus practically a ruler of the whole of Northern India except the Panjāb. Being thus a powerful monarch and practically of the same family as

[1] Pargiter, 21 & 68.

Bimbisāra, he was, in later times when the Purāṇas were recast, placed at the head of the family, and all the kings styled Śiśunāgas after him. Śiśunāga reigned for eighteen years and was succeeded by his son Aśoka. To distinguish him from Aśoka, the Maurya Emperor, he was designated Kālāśoka, the epithet *kāla* indicating his black complexion. This also explains why he was called Kākavarṇa in the Purāṇas. As a Burmese tradition informs us, he removed his capital from Rājagriha to Pāṭaliputra.[1] This is exactly in keeping with the Mahāvaṁsa,[2] which represents Kālāśoka to be established in Pushpapura, *i.e.* Pāṭaliputra. The only event which, we know, took place in the reign of Kālāśoka was the holding of the second Buddhist Council. It was held in Vesāli under this king in the year 383—2 B. C. and led to the separation of the Mahāsaṁghikas from the Theravāda[3]. Kālāśoka reigned for twenty-eight years only. After him his ten sons conjointly ruled over the Magadha empire. Their names are: (1) Bhadrasena, (2) Koraṇḍavarṇa, (3) Maṅgura, (4) Sarvañjaha, (5) Jālika, (6) Ubhaka, (7) Sañjaya, (8) Koravya, (9) Nandivardhana and (10) Pañchamaka.[4] Nandivardhana of this is most probably

---

1 SBE. XI. Intro. xvi.

2 IV. 32.

3 *Mahāvaṁsa* (trans. Geiger), Intro., lix.

4 *Mahābodhivaṁsa*, 98.

Nandivardhana of the Purāṇic list.[1] These ten brothers held joint sway over the Magadha dominions for about twenty-two years and were supplanted by the Nanda dynasty. Nine members of this dynasty are said in the Mahāvaṁsa [2] to have reigned in succession and for a period of twenty two years. They were most probably one father and eight sons as mentioned in the Purāṇas.[3] They were: (1) Ugrasena, (2) Paṇḍuka, (3) Paṇḍugati, (4) Bhūtapāla, (5) Rāshṭrapāla, (6) Govishāṇaka, (7) Daśasiddhaka, (8) Kaivarta and (9) Dhana.[4] As Ugrasena heads the list, it seems that he was the father and the remaining princes his sons. The chief of the Nandas, according to all the Purāṇas, is Mahāpadma. The commentary on the Bhāgavata-Purāṇa says that he was so called because he was the lord of soldiers or wealth numbering or amounting to 100,000 millions. Probably the correct meaning would be that he was master of as big an army as could be arrayed in a *padma-vyūha* or in a lotus fashion.[5] This agrees with the fact that in Buddhist works he has been styled Ugrasena, *i.e.* possessed of a terrific army.

---

[1] Pargiter, 22. [2] V. 15.

[3] In this respect the Purāṇas agree among themselves. They, however, differ in regard to the sequence of their rule, some saying that they all reigned conjointly, and some, in succession.

[4] *Mahābodhivaṁsa*, 98.

[5] IA., XLIV, 49-50.

The Purāṇas say that Ugrasena-Mahāpadma was so powerful that he uprooted all the Kshatriyas like Paraśurāma, brought the whole earth under one royal umbrella, and made himself *eka-rāṭ*, sole monarch. Let us pause here for a moment and see what this means. I have told you that shortly before Buddha lived, that part of India which was Aryanised was divided into sixteen different states, of which, excepting two, all were petty kingships. But the process of centralisation had begun, and we find that these tiny kingships had already developed into four monarchies in the time of Buddha. Gradually these monarchies themselves were being dissolved and coalesced into one, but they did not culminate into a full-fledged imperialism until a century after the demise of Buddha. We have seen above how the Magadha Empire gradually extended and swallowed not only the Kāsi-Kosala country of the Ikshvākus, but also the Avanti territory of the Pradyotas and the Kauśāmbī kingdom of the Vatsas. And when Ugrasena-Mahāpadma has been expressly represented by the Purāṇas to have exterminated the Kshatriyas and brought the earth under his sole sway, it means, I think, that he made himself master of about that whole portion of India which was familiar to the Aryans, *i.e.* of almost all the sixteen countries into which India was divided in Buddha's time and which I have already enumerated about the beginning of this lecture. In other words, Ugrasena-Mahāpadma was a Chakravartin or universal monarch. The idea of Chakravartin is very ancient in India. The Aitareya-Brāhmaṇa, *e.g.* makes mention of some kings, who, after their anointing, conquered the whole earth and performed a horse-sacrifice. What we have in this connection to bear in mind is that by 'earth' is meant not the whole earth as it is known to us at the present day but rather the earth as it was known to the Aryans at the time when the Chakravartin is said to have lived and conquered. Mahāpadma was thus but one Chakravartin and was the Chakravartin of the period we have selected. Kauṭilya in his Arthaśāstra[1] speaks of the Chakravartin as if the latter was not a novel ruler at all in his day and tells us that his domain coincided with the greater portion of the space between the Himālayas and the ocean and with an area of a thousand *yojanas*. This no doubt answers to the extent of the Mauryan empire, and as from the language of Kauṭilya the Chakravartin was not an unfamiliar figure in his time, it appears that there was at least one Chakravartin before the Mauryas came to power, and there is, therefore, nothing strange in our taking Mahāpadma to be a Chakravartin on

---

[1] p. 338.

the authority of the Purāṇas. It is time therefore to give up the view that the Indians for the first time gained their idea of Chakravartin from Alexander's invasion.

LECTURE III.

ADMINISTRATIVE HISTORY.

(a) *Literature on Hindu Polity.*

In this and the next lecture I propose to deal with the administrative history of the period. This history may be of two kinds: (1) history of the literature bearing upon the science and art of government and (2) history setting forth the actual practices and systems of administration prevalent in the period. The latter is not possible without the former. It is, therefore, absolutely necessary to know beforehand what sort of literature was extant in our period relating to political science, or Arthaśāstra as it was called.

South India has recently become a land of discoveries. Not many years ago the students of ancient Indian poetics were taken by surprise by the discovery of Bhāmaha's work on Alaṁkāra in Trivandrum. The dramas of Bhāsa, the celebrated dramatist who preceded Kālidāsa, had for a long time remained hidden from modern eyes until they were discovered seven years ago at the same place, *viz.* Trivandrum. Such was the case with the Arthaśāstra of Kauṭilya. That a work dealing with the science of politics was composed by Kauṭilya had been testified to by various more or less early Indian writers who have not only referred to the author but also given quotations from his work. But the work had been looked upon as entirely lost, and it was a great though agreeable surprise to every scholar and antiquarian when, in the January number of the *Indian Antiquary*, 1905, Mr. R. Shamasastry not only announced the discovery of this work at Tanjore but actually published a translation of some of its chapters. The whole book was afterwards edited and translated by the same scholar and is being more and more eagerly and thoroughly studied, but it will be still long before we are able to show what flood of light it throws not only on ancient polity but also on economics, law, ethics and so forth.

When the Arthaśāstra of Kauṭilya was first published, it evoked a great deal of criticism more or less of an adverse nature. But now there is a consensus of opinion among scholars that on the ground of the archaic style and the social and religious life depicted therein the work has certainly to be assigned to the period B.C. 321-296 as it claims to belong. Any student who has even cursorily read the book knows that it bristles with quotations from the authors of the Arthaśāstra who were prior to Kauṭilya. It therefore follows that if these authors were known to Kauṭilya, their works were certainly known and studied in the period we have selected, especially as it immediately precedes Chandragupta, the founder of the Maurya dynasty, whose prime-minister Kauṭilya was. It is therefore very important to know who are these authors that have been referred to by Kauṭilya. The list of those that I have been able to frame is as follows :—

Schools.

1. Mānavāḥ, pp. 6, 29, 63, 177, 192.
2. Bārhaspatyāḥ, pp. 6, 29, 63, 177, 192, 373.
3. Auśanasāḥ, pp. 6, 29, 63, 177, 192.
4. Pārāśarāḥ, p. 63.
5. Āmbhīyāḥ[1], p. 33.

The order in which the schools are mentioned is not uniform.

Individual Authors.

6. Bhāradvāja, pp. 13, 27, 32, 253, 320, 325, 380.
7. Viśālāksha, pp, 13, 27, 32, 320, 326, 380.
8. Parāśara[2], pp. 13, 27, 32, 321, 326.

[1] *Āmbhīyāḥ* is probably a mistake for *Āchāryāḥ*, as Prof. Jacobi thinks (*Überdie Echtheit des Kauṭilīya* in *Sitzungsberichte der Königlich Preussischen Akademie der Wissenschaften*, p. 837).

[2] His name has been variously spelt in the printed edition *Parāśaraḥ*, *Pārāśaraḥ* and *Pārāśarāḥ*. Of course, the plural form is

9. Piśuna[1], pp. 14, 28, 33, 251, 321, 327.
10. Kauṇapadanta[2], pp. 14, 33, 321, 327.
11. Vātavyādhi, pp. 14, 33, 261, 322, 328.
12. Bāhudantīputra[3], p. 14.

These authors (Nos. 6-12) are specified in the above serial order.

13. Kātyāyana,	p. 251.	These have been mentioned but once. Of these again Chārāyaṇa and Ghoṭa(ka)-mukha have been mentioned by Vātsyāyana as authors of the different parts of the Science of Erotics.
14. Kaṇiṅka Bhāradvāja	,,	
15. Dīrgha-Chārāyaṇa	,,	
16. Ghoṭamukha	,,	
17. Kiñjalka	,,	
18. Piśunaputra	,,	

---

inadmissible, where this name has been mentioned along with those of individual authors. Of the remaining two, *Parāśaraḥ* appears to me to be the correct form, because it has been so mentioned in *Kāmandaka*, VIII. 39, where, again, the metrical exigencies require *Parāśaraḥ* and not *Pārāśaraḥ*. *Pārāśaraḥ* stands in the same relation to *Pārāśarāḥ* as *Uśanāḥ* of Kāmandaka does to his *Kavayaḥ* (VIII-22 & 27).

[1] Piśuna was another name of Nārada; and we know that he was the author of a work on kingly duties from the passage *Nāradīyam=iv=āvarṇyamāna-rājadharmam* from the *Kādambarī* (Bo. Sk. Series, p. 91, l. 13). This passage cannot possibley refer to the *Nārada-Smṛiti*, because it does not deal with kingly duties.

[2] According to the *Trikāṇḍaśesha*, Kauṇapadanta is another name for Bhīshma, and it is not at all improbable that Kauṇapadanta's work is represented by the present *Rājadharm-ānuśāsana* of Bhīshma in the *Śānti-Parvan* of the Mahābhārata.

[3] The correct form of the name must be Bāhudantīputra as has been shown further on in the text.

Now the question arises have any of these names been mentioned anywhere? Those who have read the Mahābhārata need not be told that some of these certainly occur in the Śānti-Parvan. Chapter 58 of this Parvan sets forth no less than seven names of the authors of the treatises on kingly duties. They are (1) Bṛihaspati, (2) Viśālāksha, (3) Kāvya, (4) Mahendra, (5) Prāchetasa Manu, (6) Bhāradvāja and (7) Gauraśiras. Except the last, *viz.* Gauraśiras, all are identifiable with the names specified by Kauṭilya. Bṛihaspati must be the founder of the Bārhaspatya, Kāvya, the same as Śukra, of the Auśanasa, and Manu, of the Mānava, School. In regard to Manu it is to be noted that here he has been called Prāchetasa which distinguishes him from Svāyambhuva Manu, the author of the Dharmaśāstra, and from Vaivasvata Manu, the first king of the human species.[1] Bhāradvāja of the Śānti-Parvan must be the Bhāradvāja mentioned in Kauṭilya's Arthaśāstra. There thus remains one name, *viz.* Mahendra. He is identical with Bāhudantin, the first component of the name Bāhudantiputra referred to by Kauṭilya as we shall see shortly.

---

[1] In regard to Svāyambhuva Manu, the author of the Dharmaśāstra *vide Ādi-P.*, 73.9; *Śānti-P.*, 335.43. In respect of Prāchetasa Manu, *vide Śānti-P.*, 57.42, after which two verses from his *Rāja-dharmas* are quoted. In *Vana-P.*, 35, 21 also, are referred to the *Rāja-dharmas* of Manu who can, therefore, be no other than Prāchetasa. Of course, no scholar will now agree with Bühler in the view he has expressed in *SBE.*, XXV. Intro. lxxvi, n. 1.

It was indeed a wise move on the part of the Calcutta University to have prescribed for M. A. History, the chapters of the Śānti-Parvan, which treat of *Rājadharma, i.e.* the duties of the king, and which, in fact, give us good glimpses into the condition of the science of polity before the time of Kauṭilya. We have seen that Chapter 58 of this Parvan gives the names of the authors of *Rājaśāstra* which all except one agree with those mentioned by Kauṭilya. Let us now proceed a step further and see what the immediately next chapter teaches us. This chapter gives us a genesis of the science of polity—how it arose and how it underwent alterations. *Daṇḍanīti* or Science of Polity, we are told, was first brought out by Brahmā. It treated not only of the objects of the worldly life, *viz. dharma*, performance of religious duties, *artha*, attainment of wealth and *kāma*, gratification of sensual desires, but also of *moksha* or final beatitude, and consisted of one hundred thousand chapters. As the period of the human life was gradually decreasing, this colossal work was also undergoing abridgement. The god Śiva was the first to shorten it into a treatise called Vaiśālāksha after him and consisting of ten thousand chapters. The divine Indra then abridged it into a work comprising five thousand chapters and styled Bāhudantaka after him. Bṛihaspati further reduced it to a work containing three thousand chapters and designated Bārhaspatya after him. Last came Kavi or Uśanas, who still further shortened it into a treatise composed of a thousand chapters only. Now the original work composed by Brahmā is said to have treated of *dharma*, *artha*, *kāma* and *moksha*, and comprised one hundred thousand chapters. In Chapter 335 of the Śānti-Parvan we have another tradition narrated about this work. There its authorship has been ascribed to eight sages, who read it out to the god Nārāyaṇa. The god was exceedingly pleased with what he heard, and said: "Excellent is this treatise that ye have composed consisting of a hundred thousand verses...... Guided by it Svāyambhuva Manu will himself promulgate to the world its code of *dharma*, and Uśanas and Bṛihaspati compose their treatises based upon it." We are then told that this original work of the sages will last up to the time of king Uparicharu and disappear upon his death. Curiously enough, Vātsyāyana, author of the *Kāmasūtra*, mentions at the beginning of this work a third tradition which is a combination of the first two. Prajāpati or Brahmā, says he, created people and recited to them a work consisting of one hundred thousand chapters to enable them to attain *dharma*, *artha*, and *kāma*. That part which related to *dharma* was separated by Manu, and those which related to *artha* and *kāma* were separated by Bṛihaspati and Nandin respectively. We thus see that according to the tradition mentioned both in Chapter 59 of the Śānti-Parvan and by Vātsyāyana the original knowledge about the work on *dharma*, *artha* and *kāma* emanated from Brahmā. The first abridgement of Daṇḍanīti, we have seen, is ascribed to Śiva after whom it was named Vaiśālāksha. The term Vaiśālāksha is derived from Viśālāksha, which is another name for Śiva. The author Viśālāksha mentioned by Kauṭilya must therefore be taken to refer to the god Śiva himself[1]. The second abridgement was brought out by Indra, and, we are informed, was called Bāhudantaka. Indra's elephant, Airāvata, because he had four *i.e.* many (*bahu*) tusks, could be called Bahudanta

[1] It may be asked whether it is permissible to quote the views and the name of a god exactly as would be done in the case of a human being, and it may consequently be doubted whether Kauṭilya's Viśālāksha is a divinity or a human being. It may, therefore, be contended that up to Kauṭilya's time Viśālāksha was a human author but was afterwards looked upon as a god and mentioned as such in the Śānti-Parvan. We know, however, that, as a matter of fact, Kāmandaka cites the doctrines and mentions the names of Puloma and Indra, about whose divinity there can be no question, as if they were human authors, as is clear from VIII. 21. Again, nobody can doubt that the Śānti-Parvan was existing in its present form about 300 A.D, when Kāmandaka lived. To Kāmandaka, therefore, Viśālāksha must have been a god, and yet he speaks of the latter as *Viśālākshaḥ prabhāshate* (VIII. 28). No reasonable doubt need therefore be entertained as to Kauṭilya's reference to Viśālāksha being a reference to the god of that name.

or Bāhudanta; and because Indra possessed Bahudanta or Bāhudanta *i.e.* Airāvata, he could be called Bāhudanta or Bāhudantin. And it is from the first of these names that the science of polity composed by him was styled Bāhudantaka. The second name can be recognised in Bāhudantiputra mentioned by Kauṭilya. There can be no doubt that the first component of the latter is Bāhudanti°, and not Bāhudantī° *i.e.* the ending *i* is short and not long and that Bāhudanti° must here denote Indra[1]. In regard to the second component *putra*, we have got an exactly analogous case in Piśunaputra. We have seen that Kauṭilya mentions not only Piśuna but also Piśunaputra. The word *putra* in all probability signifies here 'a follower.' Thus in the Mṛichchhakaṭika those, who follow the science of theft originated by the god Kārtikeya, are called Skandaputras by Śarvilaka[2]. Bāhudantiputra must therefore denote a follower of Bāhudantin, *i.e.* of the system of the Arthaśāstra laid down by him. Piśunaputra must similarly denote a follower of the system of Piśuna or Nārada, who, we know, was an

---

[1] This, I think, is clear from the fact that Kāmandaka also speaks of Indra as one of the authors of the Arthaśāstra (*vide* the preceding note).

[2] *Mṛichchhakaṭika* (BSS), 141. The word *putra* was used to denote also the follower of a religious system. Thus *nigaṇṭha-putto* signified a Jaina (*Maj-N.* I. 227. where Sachchaka is so called).

authority on the *rāja-dharma* and is referred to by Bāṇa in his *Kādambarī*[1]. The third abridgement is attributed to Bṛihaspati and is designated Bārhaspatya. For the fourth, Kāvya or Uśanas was responsible. The name of his work is not specified, but it must have been Auśanasa. In Chapter 59 of the Śānti-Parvan we have a specific mention not only of four of the seven authors of Arthaśāstra enumerated in Chapter 58 but also of the works standing to their credit. It is somewhat curious that Manu, Bhāradvāja and Gauraśiras have here been passed away. But the probable explanation is that these were sages and consequently human beings, whereas those noticed above were either gods or demi-gods and that the object of the tradition narrated in Chapter 59 is to establish the sacred character and the extreme antiquity of the Arthaśāstra by showing how it was handed down from Brahmā through the various gods and at the same time more and more abridged in this process of transmission. Of course, Manu and his work must have been well-known at this time, for in the Droṇa-Parvan we find that one of his qualifications to become the generalissimo of the Kaurava army Droṇāchārya makes a pointed mention of his proficiency in *Mānavī*

---

[1] See p. 90, n. 2.

Artha-vidyā[1]. This clearly indicates that a work on Arthaśāstra composed by Manu was well-known, and was held in such high repute that proficiency in it was considered to be a great merit to a general. About Bhāradvāja I shall say something further in the sequel, but no reference to the work of Gauraśiras I have been able to trace in the Mahābhārata.

Now, here another question arises: have we got any evidence to show in what form the works of these ancient authors of the Arthaśāstra were composed? It is indeed a very interesting fact that Śānti-Parvan is not content with merely enumerating their names or specifying their works but actually quotes verses from the latter. Chapters 56-8 are very important in this respect. We have three verses cited not only from Manu but also from Uśanas (Bhārgava) and Bṛihaspati. These have all been culled in the Appendix. This gives rise to the inference that their works at any rate were in metrical form. And in regard to the work of Uśanas in particular, it is possible to say that it was in existence and in metrical form even as late as the time of Śaṅkarārya, commentator of the *Kāmandakīya Nītisāra*, for we know he actually quotes one verse from it.[2]

The conclusion that the works on Arthaśāstra prior to Kauṭilya were in verse is forced upon

---

[1] *IA.*, *XLVI*, 95.
[2] TSS. Ed. 112.

us by a study of the latter's work also. Before, however, this can be demonstrated, it is necessary to find out the exact nature of the form of composition which his work represents. This is described at the end of his book in the verse:

Dṛishṭvā vipratipattiṁ bahudhā śāstreshu bhāshyakārāṇām
svayam=eva Vishṇuguptaś=chakāra sūtraṁ cha bhāshyaṁ cha.

TRANSLATION.

"Having noticed discrepancy in many ways between the commentators on the Śāstras, Vishṇugupta himself has made the Sūtra and the commentary."

Unfortunately, so far as I know, the meaning of this verse has not been made clear by any scholar[1]. What the verse, however, evidently means is that in Kauṭilya's time a *Sūtra* was interpreted differently by different commentators and that in order that this mishap may not befall his work he composed not only the *Sūtras* but also the commentary setting forth his meaning of his *Sūtras*. Kauṭilya's book, therefore, consists not only of *Sūtra* but also of

[1] Prof. Jacobi explains it in a different manner (loc. cit 843 & 845). Although the verse in question distinctly says that Kauṭilya's work is both a Sūtra and a Bhāshya, he seems to think it, apparently on the authority of the same verse, that it is, not a Sūtra, but rather a Bhāshya!

Bhāshya. It is a matter of regret, however, that in the edition published of his Arthaśāstra, the *Sūtra* has not been separated from the *Bhāshya.* I will explain myself more clearly. Take *e.g.* pp. 27-8 which deal with the subject of *Mantr-ādhikāra.* Here as elsewhere the *Sūtra* and the *Bhāshya* have been hopelessly intermixed so that the ordinary reader does not know that part of what he reads is the *Sūtra* and part the *Bhāshya.* I will extricate the *Sūtras* of these pages to show that whatever remains is the *Bhāshya.* The *Sūtras* here are as follows :

(1) *Guhyam=eko mantrayet=eti Bhārad-vājaḥ*

(2) *N=aikasya mantra-siddhir=ast=īti Viśālākshaḥ*

(3) *Etan=mantra-jñānaṁ n=aitan=man-tra-rakshaṇam=iti Pārāśaraḥ*

(4) *N=eti Piśunaḥ*

(5) *N=eti Kauṭilyaḥ*

(6) *Mantribhis=tribhiś=chaturbhir=vā saha mantrayeta*

and so on.

These are the *Sūtras*, and whatever is published in the book along with each *Sūtra* so as to form a paragraph is the *Bhāshya.* There is yet another element of this work which requires to be considered—I mean the verses which are as a rule given at the end of each chapter. Who can be the author of these verses ? Were they all composed by Kauṭilya himself ? Let us try to answer this question. There can be no doubt that some at least were composed by him. Certainly the first two of the verses occurring on p. 17 of the published text must belong to him. The first gives the opinion of the previous *Āchāryas* that the king shall employ his ministers in offices corresponding to their ascertained purity. The second cites the view of Kauṭilya that the king shall in no wise test their purity on himself or his queen. The phrase here used is *etat Kauṭilya-darśanam*. This indicates that these two verses at any rate come from the pen of Kauṭilya. And we can suppose that there were perhaps some others which also were composed by him. It is not however, possible to concede more and assert that he was the author of all the verses met with in his work. This is strongly negatived by the fact that on pp. 365-6 occur two stanzas[1] with the prefatory remark : *ap=īha ślokau bhavataḥ*. This is an unmistakable indication that these verses at any rate were not of Kauṭilya, but were quoted by him from some work. Again, we have at least two instances of verses prefaced by one or more words in prose either of which is insufficient by itself but which

[1] The second of these stanzas occurs also in the *Pratijñā-Yaugandharāyaṇa* (TSS.Ed., 62), and the first in the *Parāśara-dharma-saṁhitā* (BSS. Ed. I. ii. 272).

together make the sense whole and complete. Thus on p. 121 we have the following :

Surakāmedak-ārishta-madhu-phal-āmlāmla-śīdhūnāṁ cha—

Ahnaś=cha vikrayaṁ vyājiṁ jñātvā māna-hiraṇyayoḥ
tathā vaidharaṇaṁ kuryād=uchitaṁ ch=ānuvartayet

Here the verse by itself does not bring out the full sense, which is possible only when it is interpreted in conjunction with the preceding prose line. Similar is the case on p. 29 where we have the following :

Kurvataś=cha—

N=āsya guhyaṁ pare vidyuś=chhidraṁ vidyāt parasya cha
gūhet kūrma iv=āṅgāni yat syād=vivṛitam=ātmanaḥ

Here the verse is preceded by two words in prose which together make clear the sense of the author. Now this practice of combining a verse with a prose passage to express an idea is often met with in Sanskrit dramas where it is indispensable for dramatic effect, but is conspicuous by its absence in any work dealing with a *Śāstra* when the whole of it is a production of one author. In a work setting forth the subject of a *Śāstra* no dramatic effect is ever intended, and when therefore we meet with such a combination of prose and verse, the only reasonable conclusion is that the author is citing that verse from some other source and that in order to fully bring out its sense he has to preface it with a remark of his in prose. The two verses given above must, therefore, be supposed as not belonging to Kauṭilya but rather quoted by him from a previous work on Arthaśāstra. There is yet another line of argument which compels us to adopt the same conclusion. The second of the verses just quoted from Kauṭilya occurs also in the Śānti-Parvan. I am aware one is apt to suspect that the Śānti-Parvan is indebted to Kauṭilya for this verse. But this is not possible, because I have just shown that it cannot belong to Kauṭilya as it is preceded by a prose preface. But there are other considerations also which leave no scepticism on this point. The verse in question, *viz.* that beginning with *n=āsya guhyaṁ pare vidyuḥ* occurs not only in the Śānti but also in the Ādi-Parvan. But here it is preceded by two verses which run thus :

Nityam=udyata-daṇḍaḥ syān=nityaṁ
vivṛita-paurushaḥ
achchhidraś=chhidra-darśī syāt pareshāṁ
vivar-ānugaḥ
Nityam=udyata-daṇḍād=hi bhṛiśam=
udvijate janaḥ
tasmāt sarvāṇi kāryāṇi daṇḍen=aiva vi-
dhārayet

Now, all these three verses, it is worthy of note, occur in Chapter VII of the Manu-smṛiti. The question, therefore, arises: who borrowed from whom? Fortunately for us this question has been threshed out by no less an illustrious scholar than Prof. Bühler[1]. The above are not the only verses that are common to the Mahābhārata and the Manu-smṛiti. There are many others which have been pointed out by him in the introduction to his translation of the Manu-smṛiti, and on a careful consideration of the question he has expressed the view that the editor of this metrical *Smṛiti* has not drawn upon the Mahābhārata or *vice versa* but that the authors of both works have utilised the materials that already existed. It is thus plain that the verse *n=āsya guhyaṁ pare vidyuḥ* etc. was not composed by Kauṭilya but was utilised by him from some work which was in existence long before he wrote or the Śānti-Parvan or the Manu-smṛiti was compiled[2].

It will be perceived that all the verses except a few ones that occur in Kauṭilya's Arthaśāstra

---

[1] *SBE.*, XXV., Intro. xc.

[2] One more verse from Kauṭilya is worth considering in this connection. It occurs on p. 217, and begins with *saṁvatsareṇa patati*. The same verse is met with in Manu, XI. 180, Vāsishṭha, I. 22 and Baudhāyana, II. i. 35. As there were some subjects common to the Arthaśāstra and the Dharmaśāstra, it is very difficult to say whether Kauṭilya borrowed the verse from some work on the Dharmaśāstra, such as Manu, Vasishṭha or Baudhāyana or from some work on the Arthaśāstra. Of course, the name *Dharmaśāstra* was known to Kauṭilya (p. 10).

have been quoted by him from previous authors. When we, therefore, find any verses cited along with and in confirmation of the doctrines set forth by him of his predecessors, the natural conclusion is that the verses in question were quoted from the works of the latter. Such verses do we find *e.g.* on pages 13, 27 and 253 of the printed edition. This shows that the works of Bhāradvāja, Viśālāksha and Parāśara at least were in metrical form. In the case of Bhāradvāja the matter has been placed beyond all doubt, because Kauṭilya actually cites part of a verse and ends the quotation with the remark *iti Bhāradvājaḥ*. I am, of course, referring here to *Indrasya hi sa praṇamati yo balīyaso namati iti Bhāradvājaḥ* on p. 380. This quotation, I need scarcely say, forms the second half of an Āryā verse, and is exceedingly interesting inasmuch as it shows that in the earlier works on Arthaśāstra, not only the Anushṭubh but also the Āryā metre was employed. We have already seen on the authority of the Mahābhārata that the works on polity attributed to Manu, Bṛihaspati and Uśanas were in verse, and we now see on the authority of Kauṭilya that the same was the case with the works of Bhāradvāja, Viśālāksha and Parāśara.

Here the question may be asked: how is it possible to regard the works on Arthaśāstra anterior to Kauṭilya as being metrical in form when the work of the latter, as we have seen, belongs to the Sūtra class of composition? Does it not conflict with the established opinion of the Sanskritists that a Sūtra work is prior to a work in which the Anushṭubh metre is uniformly employed? I admit that this opinion is at present highly countenanced by scholars, but I dispute its correctness. It was Max Müller[1] who first gave utterance to this view, which has now been followed rather slavishly by Sanskritists in spite of the strong protest raised against it by Goldstücker[2]. The latter scholar clearly tells us that it is one thing to lay down a criterion by which a class of works such *e.g.* as the Sūtras might become recognisable, and it is another thing to make such a criterion a basis for computing periods of literature and that two classes of writings can flourish in one and the same period; and, as a matter of fact, he has clearly proved that the Anushṭubh or metrical form of composition was existing side by side with the Sūtra in that very period to which the latter style of literature has been assigned. Which class of composition began earlier—the Sūtra or the metrical—is a question which need not trouble us here. My contention is that from the 7th century B. C. onwards to the time of Kauṭilya both the forms of composition flourished

---

[1] HASL., 68 & ff.

[2] Pāṇini, 78 & ff.

side by side as has been well shown by Goldstücker, and there can, therefore, be nothing strange in the Arthaśāstra works of the pre-Kauṭilyan period being metrical in form although they pertain to the period to which the Sūtra class of literature is generally ascribed and although the work of Kauṭilya himself is an example of this class.

Many of the chapters of the Śānti-Parvan narrate incidents in the form of dialogues which are designated *purātana itihāsa*. Most of these *itihāsas* relate to matters connected with Dharma, Purāṇa and so forth. But at least two relate to the *Arthaśāstra*. One of these is set forth in Chapter 68, where we are introduced to a discourse between Bṛihaspati and Vasumanas, king of Kosala. Vasumanas pays his homage to the great sage, and enquires about the governance of a kingdom, and Bṛihaspati replies by dwelling on the paramount necessity of having a king at the head of the State. In the course of his discourse Bṛihaspati likens a king to the gods Agni, Āditya, Mṛityu, Vaiśravaṇa and Yama, and a verse is given, *viz. Na hi jātv=avamantavyo manushya iti bhūmipaḥ* । *mahatī devatā hy=eshā nara-rūpeṇa tishṭhati* ॥ 40 ॥ which we find also in Manu (VII, 8). Then in Chapter 140 of the same Parvan we are introduced to another dialogue, this time between the sage Bhāradvāja and Śatruñjaya, king of Sauvīra. King Śatruñjaya puts Bhāradvāja a question contained in the verse : *Alabdhasya kathaṁ lipsā labdhaṁ kena vivardhate । vardhitaṁ pālyate kena pālitaṁ praṇayet katham* ॥ 5 ॥ which forms the very essence of the Science of Polity according to Kauṭilya, as is clear from his words : *(Daṇḍanītiḥ) alabdha-lābh-ārthā labdha-parirakshaṇī rakshita-vivardhanī vṛiddhasya tīrtheshu pratipādanī cha.*[1] Bhāradvāja's reply commences with the two verses, one beginning with *Nityam=uddyata-daṇḍaḥ syāt* and theother with *Nityam=uddyata-daṇḍasya* followed soon by the third verse whose second half is *gūhet kūrma iv=āṅgāni etc.*, exactly the three verses quoted on pages 1 1-2 above as being common to the Ādi-Parvan and the Manu-smṛiti. From these data it is not unreasonable, I hope, to draw the following inferences : (1) Just as in the case of every Purāṇa we are informed of the occasion on which and the people to whom and the person by whom it was recited, it seems that at the outset of each Arthaśāstra were specified the occasion which led to its exposition and the sage by.whom and the person or persons for whose edification it was discoursed.[2] This explains why Kauṭilya places Arthaśāstra, like Purāṇa and Dharmaśāstra,

---

[1] p. 9.

[2] The Auśanasa Arthaśāstra similarly seems to have been a discourse of the sage Uśanas to Pralhāda (*Śānti-P.*, 139. 69).

under Itihāsa[1]. (2) It appears that the works named after Bṛihaspati and Bhāradvāja at any rate were not composed by them but rather embodied the doctrines expounded by them orally to certain kings and on certain occasions. (3) The verse 40, cited from Chapter 68 of the Śānti-Parvan, which we find is practically identical with Manu, VII. 8, (p. 106), must, therefore, be supposed to have originally belonged to the work setting forth the system of Bṛihaspati. For the same reason Bhāradvāja must be supposed to be the author of the three verses quoted from Chapter 140 of the same Parvan and shown to be identical with Manu, VII. 102-3 and 105[2] (p. 107).

When Kauṭilya wrote, the study of the Arthaśāstra was falling into desuetude. This, I think, is clear from one of the verses occurring at the end of his book, *viz*:

---

[1] P. 10.

[2] Like Arthaśāstra Kauṭilya (p. 10) places Dharmaśāstra also under Itihāsa. I suspect that Dharmaśāstra, too, like Arthaśāstra, was originally of metrical composition before it assumed the Sūtra form. This alone can explain, I think, why verses have been introduced into the Dharmasūtras, just as they are in Kauṭilīya. As in the latter case we know they were borrowed from previous works on Arthaśāstra, those in the Dharmasūtras must similarly have been borrowed from previous works of that science which must therefore be supposed to have been metrical in form. And I suspect that the original Manusmṛiti, and, not the present recast one, was prior even to the Dharmasūtras, especially as verses from the latter have been traced to the former; *vide* also p. 113, n. 2 below. I hope I may find time once to work out this theory fully.

Yena śāstraṁ cha śastraṁ cha
Nanda-rāja-gatā cha bhūḥ
amarsheṇ=oddhṛitāny=āśu
tena śāstram=idaṁ kṛitam.

This verse is evidently crediting Kauṭilya with having rescued Śāstra, which can here mean Arthaśāstra only[1]. It thus seems that the old works on the Arthaśāstra were being forgotten in his time. And to rescue this Science from oblivion Kauṭilya appears to have made a vigorous attempt at getting hold of the old works, most of which he did succeed in obtaining and which he brought into requisition in composing his treatise. And we know what a stupendous mass of literature it was. There were, to begin with, at least four Schools connected with this Science. A School means a traditional handing down of a set of doctrines and presupposes a series of *āchāryas* or teachers, who from time to time carried on the work of exegetics and systematisation. Besides, we find that Kauṭilya mentions not only four Schools but also thirteen individual authors who were in no way connected with any School. Again, we have already seen that of the teachers of our Science referred to in the Śānti-Parvan all except one have been mentioned by Kauṭilya. This exception was Gauraśiras, whose work

[1] The word *uddhṛita* is taken in the sense of 'reformed' by Prof. Jacobi (loc. cit 837), which is scarcely admissible, I am afraid.

[2] *Kauṭilīya*, pp. 7 & 10.

perhaps seems to have been lost in his time. It is quite possible that there may have been works of some more teachers which were similarly forgotten, especially as we have seen that in Kauṭilya's time the Science of Polity was being well-nigh extinct. The latest of these works again must for the same reason be supposed to have been written at least three-quarters of a century anterior to his time. All things considered, it is impossible to bring down the beginning of Indian thought in the sphere of Arthaśāstra to any period later than 650 B.C. We have seen that Chapter 59 of the Śānti-Parvan attributes the origin of this Science to the god Brahmā and of the different treatises on it to the different gods and demi-gods. This means that in the 4th century B.C. Arthaśāstra was looked upon as having come from such a hoary antiquity that it was believed to have emanated from the divine, and not from the human, mind. This agrees with the fact that in Kauṭilya's time Arthaśāstra was comprised in Itihāsa, which was then looked upon as a Veda and of the same dignity as the Atharva-Veda.[1]

We thus see that much of the matter supplied by Kauṭilya's work pertains to the period selected by us, and can be safely used to show how much the Indians knew of this science in that period. To the same period seem to belong the chapters

---

[1] *Kauṭilīya*, 7.

from the Mahābhārata, especially from the Śānti-Parvan, which deal with *rājadharm-ānu-śāsana*; and it is not at all improbable that this section represents in the main the work of the pre-Kauṭilyan political philosopher Kauṇapadanta as this is but another name for Bhīshma. The account of polity which they contain seems to have been drawn principally from the systems of Bṛihaspati, Uśanas and Manu. Again, when those chapters were written, only seven authors of this Science were known. In Kauṭilya's time they were at least twelve[1]. Again, the name

[1] It has been stated above that the order in which Kauṭilya mentions the first seven of the individual authors of the Arthaśāstra is uniform. This no doubt raises the presumption that he would have us believe that they lived in that chronological sequence, and apparently receives confirmation from the fact that thrice (on pp. 13-4, 27-8 & 32-3) Kauṭilya mentions them in such a way as to show that the doctrines of one are refuted by his immediate successor in that order of specification. There are, on the other hand, some weighty considerations which run counter to this theory. On p. 320 & ff., Kauṭilya says that of the calamities pertaining to the seven Prakṛitis or components of Sovereignty, *viz.* (1) *svāmī*, (2) *amātya*, (3) *janapada*, (4) *durga*, (5) *kośa*, (6) *daṇḍa* and (7) *mitra*, the first is more serious than its immediate second, according to the Āchāryas or the recognised authorities on the Arthaśāstra. This is not, however, the view of Bhāradvāja, Viśalāksha, Parāśara, Piśuna, Kauṇapadanta and Vātavyādhi, who are mentioned in this specific order by Kautilya. Of (1) and (2), (2) is more serious than (1) with Bhāradvāja; of (2) and (3), (3) is more serious than (2) with Viśālāksha, and so on and so on. It will be seen that the order in which the Seven Prakṛitis are enumerated is fixed by the Āchāryas who are different from Bhāradvāja, Viśālāksha and so forth. And what I cannot therefore under stand is how the six consecutive pairs (1)-(2), (2)-(3) and so forth of this series come to be taken up respectively by the six consecutive authors of Kauṭilya's enumeration. Are we to suppose that through

Gauraśiras, which is mentioned in the Śānti-Parvan, is not known to Kauṭilya showing probably that his work was forgotten when the prime-minister of Chandragupta wrote. Moreover, as the Mahābhārata does not know many of the authors adverted to by Kauṭilya, it is no wonder that it mentions none of the later authors such as Maharshis,[1] Maya and Puloma who came into prominence after him and are referred to by Kāmandaka[2].

some inexorable destiny Bhāradvāja, because he came first, had to take up for the discussion of relative importance the first pair only and then there was a lull till Viśālāksha appeared, and just because he was the second, he too had to take up the second and the second pair only, and so on and so on? Again, on p. 325 and ff. the same unalterable necessity seems to have assigned the question of relative heinousness between the *Kopajāḥ* and *Kāmajāḥ doshāḥ* to Bhāradvāja because he came first. Then it appears there was a truce for some time to further discussion till Viśālāksha the second arose. Then it was felt necessary to deduce two pairs out of the three *Kopajāḥ doshāḥ*, assign the first of these to Viśālāksha, and reserve the second till the advent of his successor, Parāśara, and so on and so on. Surely historical development of the Arthaśāstra could not have taken place according to this exact unalterable programme.

[1] By *Maharshis* we perhaps have to understand here the eight sages to whom the original work on polity has been attributed in Chapter 335 of the Śānti-Parvan. The name Maya suggests the Asura Maya, the Architect, referred to in the Sabhā-Parvan.

[2] VIII. 20-1 & 23. I need scarcely say that this Kāmandaka cannot be identified with the sage Kāmandaka mentioned in the *Śānti-P.*, 123, 10 & ff., as this would bring the final redaction of the Mahābhārata down to the 7th century A.D.—which is an impossibility. This chapter sets forth a dialogue between Kāmandaka and Aṅgarishṭha, but, as a matter of fact, we do not hear of the latter at all in Kāmandaka's Arthaśāstra. Secondly, in this chapter Kāmandaka is discoursing on a religious subject which has hardly anything to do with the Arthaśāstra and absolutely nothing with the peculiar doctrines of Kāmandaka, the political philosopher.

These considerations show that those portions of the Mahābhārata, and especially of the Śānti-Parvan, which treat of the Science of Polity, are on the whole indebted for their account to authors who lived prior to Kauṭilya. I have shown above which verses are quoted in the Mahābhārata and from which of these authors. But there seem also to be verses in this epic which are paraphrases of the original of these authors. I shall give only one, but typical, instance here. I informed you a short time ago that Kauṭilya quoted the second half of an Āryā metre from Bhāradvāja, *viz. Indrasya hi sa praṇamati yo balīyaso namati.* Now in the Mahābhārata, both in the Uddyoga and the Śānti-Parvan, we find an Anushṭubh which is an obvious rendering of this half of the Āryā verse of Bhāradvāja, *viz*:

Etay=opamayā vīra saṁnameta balīyasē
Indrāya sa praṇamate namate yo balīyase[1].

We can easily infer that the Mahābhārata must contain many such metrical adaptations of verses from works on Arthaśāstra anterior to Kauṭilya[2].

---

[1] *Uddyoga-P.*, 33.36; *Śānti-P.*, 67.11.

[2] The same is the case with the Manusmṛiti, some *ślokas* from which are reproduced in the Mahābhārata *verbatim* and some freely rendered in verse. This does not therefore warrant the conclusion as has been drawn by some scholars that that part of the epic which agrees most closely in its citations with the code of Manu is later than that portion which does not coincide. n my opinion, it rather points to the inference that the portion that co cides may be as old as that which does not.

(*b*) *Hindu conceptions of Monarchy.*

So much for the literature bearing upon Arthaśāstra. I will now turn to some subjects connected with Administration which have a greater and general interest for us all. Let us see first what were the various forms of government prevalent at this time. The principal of these, of course, were monarchy and *Gaṇa* or *Saṅgha* Government. The former was a rule by one person, and the latter by many. The royal dynasties of the Magadha, Kośala, Avanti and Vatsa countries, which I described in my last lecture, represent the monarchical form of government. In that lecture I drew your attention also to two tribes—the Lichchhavis and the Mallas, which were brought under subjection by Ajātaśatru. They are in Buddhist literature described as *Gaṇas* or *Saṅghas*. In this lecture I shall confine myself to the first form of government only, *viz.* Monarchy, and shall treat of the other in my next. In regard to Monarchy many interesting details are supplied by Hindu works on administration, but here I shall take up only those which appear to be important to me.

Now, why is a king required? Where was the necessity of a king at the helm of State affairs? Let us see what reply is given to this question by the Hindu science of polity. Chapter 67 of the Śānti-Parvan contains the following typical verses bearing on the question.

"For these reasons men desirous of prosperity should crown some person as their king. They, who live in countries where anarchy prevails cannot enjoy their wealth and wives (v. 12).

"During times of anarchy, the sinful man derives great pleasure by plundering the wealth of other people. When, however, his (ill-got) wealth is snatched away by others, he wishes for a king (v. 13).

"It is evident, therefore, that in times of anarchy the very wicked even cannot be happy. The wealth of one is snatched away by two. That of these two is snatched away by many acting together (v. 14).

"He who is not a slave is made a slave. Women, again, are forcibly abducted. For these reasons the gods created kings for protecting the people (v. 15)

"If there were no king on earth for wielding the rod of chastisement, the strong would then have preyed on the weak after the manner of fishes in the water (v. 16)"

These verses set forth the reasons why a king is indispensable. Their essence is, however, concentrated in the last verse which tells us that if there were no king, the strong would devour the weak just as the fishes do in water, and refers to what is popularly known as the *Mātsya-nyāya.* This seems to have been a very favourite maxim with the Hindu writers on the political science and is constantly repeated when they have to explain the necessity of placing a king at the head of government. Thus the Manu-smṛiti gives the following verse :

Yadi na praṇayed=rājā daṇḍaṁ
daṇḍyeshv=atandritaḥ
jale matsyān=iv=āhiṁsyan
durbalān balavattarāḥ.
Chapter VII. v. 20.

TRANSLATION.

"If the king did not unwearisomely exercise the chastising rod on those deserving to be chastised, the stronger would kill the weaker like fish in water."

Kauṭilya also gives the same illustration not once but twice in his Arthaśāstra. Thus on p. 9 he says: *Apraṇīto hi Mātsya-nyāyam=udbhāvayati balīyān=abalaṁ hi grasate daṇḍadhar-ābhāve.* "Because, if the chastising rod is not exercised, it brings about the realisation of the proverb of the greater fish swallowing the smaller. In the absence of the wielder of the chastising rod, the strong devours the weak." Here the employment of the word *daṇḍa* and the phrase *Mātsya-nyāya* and, above all, the use of the word *apraṇīta*, are all but conclusive in showing that when Kauṭilya wrote that passage, he had in mind the verse quoted above which must therefore be supposed to have been incorporated into the Manu-smṛiti from some older text of the Arthaśāstra. *Mātsya-nyāya* is again alluded to by Kauṭilya on p. 22, but as I am citing the whole passage further on and very shortly, I refrain from doing so here and content myself with saying that Kauṭilya twice speaks of the *Mātsya-nyāya* when he has to describe the anarchy that prevails in default of a king. Curiously enough this *Mātsya-nyāya* has been alluded to even in the Rāmāyaṇa when the condition is described of an *arājaka janapada*, *i.e.* a country without a king. Thus we have the verse:

N=ārājake janapade svakaṁ bhavati kasyachit
matsyā iva janā nityaṁ bhakshayanti parasparam.

Ayodhyā-kāṇḍa, Chap. 67. v. 31.

TRANSLATION.

"In a country where there is no king, nobody possesses anything which is his own. Like the fish the people are always devouring one another."

Other reasons have been set forth in the Ayodhyā-kāṇḍa of the Rāmāyaṇa from where the above verse has been extracted, pointing to the paramount necessity of appointing a king. And it is very strange that most of them are precisely the same as those adduced in Chap. 68 of the Śānti-Parvan, showing that either one has borrowed from the other or, what is more probable, both of them drew upon some previous source. I fear it will be exceedingly irksome to you if I quote all these passages from both the works, and institute a comparison between them. Besides, such a thing is not at all necessary to my main purpose, which is simply to impress upon your mind the fact that the most favourite illustration given to describe the state of a country without a ruler is that of the fish preying upon one another. This idea seems to have been so thoroughly assimilated by the Hindus that we find it repeated everywhere. Even the Khālimpur copperplate charter of Dharmapāla of the Pāla dynasty, the contents of which most of you here in Bengal must be acquainted with, refers to the *Mātsya-nyāya* while speaking of Dharmapāla's father, Gopāla. Thus we have :—

Mātsya-nyāyam=apohitum prakṛitibhir=
Lakshmyāḥ karaṁ grāhitaḥ
Śrī-Gopāla iti kshitīśa-śirasāṁ chūḍāmaṇis=
tat-sutaḥ[1]

---

[1] EI., IV. 248 & 251.

Let us now see what notions of kingship there were in our period, in other words, what theories were prevalent in regard to the origin of kingship. The first theory that I shall here allude to is that of the Social Contract. The theory in Europe was, we know, originated by Hobbes and further developed or rather altered by Locke and Rousseau. So much do we read and hear of this view while studying European History that we are apt to suppose that a mental restlessness in this sphere was confined to Europe only and never manifested itself in the political horizon of ancient India. A study of the Arthaśāstra, however, will soon disillusion our mind. The theory of Social Contract was certainly known to Kauṭilya, and is referred to by him with approval and as being handed down to his time from time previous. "People afflicted with anarchy", says he, "consequent upon the *Mātsya-nyāya*, *i.e.* the practice of the bigger fish swallowing the smaller, first elected Manu, son of Vivasvat, to be their king. They allotted one sixth of their grains and one tenth of their merchandise as his share. Subsisting on this wage kings become capable of giving safety and security to their subjects and removing their sins. Hence hermits, too, provide the king with one sixth of the grains gleaned by them, saying to themselves 'it is a tax payable to him who protects us'." The same story is repeated but at greater length in chapter 67 of the Śānti-Parvan.[1] I need not tell you that in this as in other chapters on *Rājadharma* Bhīshma is issuing instructions to Yudhishṭhira. And in Chapter 67 Bhīshma says that formerly men, being without a king, met with destruction, devouring one another like fish in water. They then assembled together, prepared a code of laws and proceeded to Brahmā, saying: "Without a king, O divine lord, we are going to destruction. Appoint some one as our king! All of us shall worship him and he shall protect us!" Thus solicited, Brahmā asked Manu, but Manu would not assent to the proposal. "I fear," said he, "all sinful acts. To govern a kingdom is exceedingly difficult, especially among men who are always false and deceitful in their behaviour." The inhabitants of the Earth then said to him: "Don't fear! The sins that men commit will touch those only that commit them. For the increase of thy treasury, we will give thee a fiftieth part of our animals and precious metals and a tenth part of our grains."[2] Thus addressed, Manu agreed, and he made his round through the world, checking wickedness everywhere and setting all men to their respective duties.

---

[1] It is worthy of note that this story occurs in all the recensions of the Mahābhārata. It must, therefore, be of a very early origin.

[2] These differ from the dues which men promised to pay to Manu according to the version of Kauṭilya. This shows that the Śānti-Parvan could not have borrowed the tradition from Kauṭilya.

A similar conception of the origin of monarchy is traceable in Buddhist literature also. The *Aggañña-suttanta* of the Dīgha-Nikāya[1] of the Southern Buddhists describes at great length the evolution of man and society and tells us how mankind was righteous to begin with, how gradually and in diverse ways sinfuless crept into human society, and how theft, lying, reviling and assaulting became rife. Thereupon men assembled together, and after taking counsel, selected the most handsome gracious and powerful individual from amongst them, addressing him thus: "Come here, O being! Do punish, revile and exile those who well deserve to be punished, reviled and exiled. We will give you a portion of our rice." He undertook the performance of this duty and received three different appellations in consequence. Because he was selected by all men (*mahājana-sammata*), he was called Mahāsammata. Because he was the lord of all fields (*khettānaṁ patīti*), he was called Kshatriya. And because he delighted others through righteousness (*dhammena pare rañjetīti*),[2] he was called Rājan. Practically the same story is repeated in

[1] III. 92 and ff. This may also be compared to the beginning of the Ulūka-Jātaka (*Jāt.* II. 352.)

[2] This agrees with the etymology of the word given in the *Śānti-P.*, 59-125.

the Mahāvastu[1], a canonical work of the North Buddhists, and this conception of kingship seems to have so deeply permeated the Buddhist community that the story of Mahā-sammata is narrated also in the post-canonical literature and of such widely separated countries as Ceylon, Burma and Tibet.[2]

From the above accounts it will be seen that sovereignty originated in a social contract. Human beings, we learn, were fighting with one another, by each person taking for himself all that he could. The state of nature was therefore a state of war, which came to an end only when men agreed to give their liberty into the hands of a sovereign. I need not tell you that this view of the origin of society bears a remarkably close correspondence with that propounded by Hobbes. But Hobbes expounded this notion of Agreement by saying that absolute power was thereby irrevocably transferred to the ruler. Such was not, however, the case with the Social Contract theory advocated by the Hindu Arthaśāstra. According to the latter the king was still the servant of the people. The sixth part of the grains and the tenth part of the merchandise that was his due

---

[1] (Senart's Edition), I, 347-8.

[2] Spence Hardy's *Manual of Buddhism*, 128; Burmese *Damathat* Richardson's Ed.) 7; Rockhill's *Life of the Buddha*, 1-9.

was but the wage that he received for his service to the people. This is the view not only of Kauṭilya and the Śānti-Parvan but also of the authorities on the Dharmaśāstra. Baudhāyana *e. g.* who flourished in the fifth century B. C. says, *shaḍ-bhāga-bhṛito rājā rakshet prajām,* "Let the king protect (his) subjects, receiving as his pay a sixth part (of their grains)."[1] In another place in the Śānti-Parvan[2] such sources of a king's revenue as the sixth part of the yield of the soil, fines and imposts to which he is entitled according to the scriptures, have been called his *vetana*, his wage, for the protection he vouchsafes to his subjects. Nay, the king is exhorted in unmistakable language that if he is unable to restore to any subject of his the wealth that has been stolen away by thieves he should compensate him from his own treasury or with wealth obtained from his dependents.[3] This was also laid down by Kauṭilya. "Whatever of the property of the citizens", says he, "robbed by thieves the king cannot recover, shall be made good from his own pocket".[4] This was also the view of the Dharma-śāstrakāras. Gautama[5] *e.g.* says that "having recovered property stolen by thieves,

[1] I. 10.1.
[2] 71.10.
[3] 75.10.
[4] p. 190.
[5] X. 46-7; cf. also *Vishṇu*, III. 66—7.

the king shall return it to the owner, or (if the stolen property is not recovered) he shall pay (its value) out of his treasury." It will thus be seen that whatever the king received by way of taxation prescribed by scriptures was considered as his wage for the service rendered by him to the people and that he was compelled to make good from his pocket any loss that his subjects suffered from their stolen property not being recovered. The king's power can thus hardly be supposed to be absolute. And it is this feature that distinguishes the Hindu theory of Social Contract from that propounded by Hobbes, and marks its superiority over the latter. The king, according to the Hindu notion, thus never wielded any unqualified power, but was looked upon as merely a public servant though of the highest order.

So much in regard to the theory of the Social Covenant so far as it was known to the early authors of the Arthaśāstra. The other theory that we now consider is that which ascribes divine origin to kingship. This theory has been set forth in Chapter 59 of the Śānti-Parvan. Yudhishṭhira begins by asking Bhīshma a most sensible question. "Whence arose the word *rājan*," interrogates Yudhishṭhira "which is used on earth? Possessed of hands, arms and neck like others, having an understanding and senses like those of others, subject like others to the same kinds of joy and grief,......in fact, similar to others in respect of all the attributes of humanity, for what reason does one man, *viz.* the king, govern the rest of the world? Why do all men seek to obtain his favour?" This was the question asked by Yudhisṭhira. To this Bhīshma gives the following reply. In the Kṛita age there was no sovereignty, no king. All men used to protect one another righteously. Soon after they were assailed by *moha* or infatuation. And in its train followed *lobha*, greed, wrath and *rāga* or unrestrained sexual indulgence. Confusion thus set in, and the Vedas (*Brahman*) and righteousness (*Dharma*) were lost. The gods were overcome with fear, and repaired to the god Brahmā. "O Lord of the three Worlds," said they, "we are about to descend to the level of human beings! Men used to pour upwards while we used to pour downwards. In consequence, however, of the cessation of all pious rites among men, great distress will be our lot." Thus addressed the god composed the treatise consisting of a hundred thousand chapters and treating of *dharma*, *artha*, *kāma* and *moksha* to which I have already referred. The gods then approached Vishṇu, the lord of creation (*prajāpati*), and said unto him—'Indicate, O god, that one among mortals who deserves to have superiority over the rest.' The god Nārāyaṇa created, by a fiat of his will, a son born of his *tejas* or lustre, named Virajas. It was, however, the seventh descendant from Vishṇu, who was crowned king and ruled according to the *daṇḍa-nīti* composed by the god Brahmā. His name was Pṛithu Vainya, and his coronation was celebrated not only by Brāhmaṇs and Ṛishis but also deities with Indra, Regents of the world, and, above all, Vishṇu himself. The eternal Vishṇu confirmed Pṛithu's power, telling him: "No one, O King, shall transcend thee." The divine Vishṇu entered the personality of that monarch, and for this reason, the entire universe offered divine worship to Pṛithu. Since that time there has been no difference between a *deva* and a *naradeva* : between a god and a human god, *i.e.* between a god and a king. And we are further told that a person, upon the exhaustion of his merit, comes down from heaven to earth and takes birth as a king conversant with *Daṇḍa-nīti* and is really portion of Vishṇu on earth. He is thus established by the gods, and no one can, therefore, transcend him. It is for this reason that the multitude obey his words of command, though he belongs to the same world and is possessed of similar limbs.

It will be seen that according to this theory the pre-social condition was one of peace and freedom. When *moha* or infatuation took possession of the human beings, confusion arose, and the gods, being alarmed, went to Prajāpati Vishṇu who directed his son Virajas to rule over men. It was, however, Pṛithu Vainya seventh descendant from Vishṇu, who was crowned king not only by gods but also by Vishṇu. Not only Pṛithu but also kings since that time are looked upon as part of Vishṇu and are therefore called *Nara-devas*, *i.e.* gods in human form. The rudiments of this notion of kingship are traceable even in the Śatapatha-Brāhmaṇa. Let me here quote a passage from this work, bearing on the point. "And as to why a Rājanya shoots, he, the Rājanya, is most manifestly of Prajāpati : hence, while being one, he rules over many."[1] The last sentence is very significant. This precisely forms the basis of the question which Yudhishṭhira asks Bhīshma at the beginning of Chapter 59 whose summary I have just given. The question is : the king is but one of the many human beings and how is it that he rules over them? Bhīshma's reply is that the king is a *nara-deva* being part of Prajāpati Vishṇu. This is just what the Śatapatha-Brāhmaṇa says. It is true that this Brāhmaṇa represents a king to be part of Prajāpati only and makes no mention of Vishṇu, but then we must remember that the

---

[1] V. 1.5.14.

same Brāhmaṇa[1] mentions Prajāpati as an epithet of the god Savitṛi who and Vishṇu represent one and the same Sun deity. This view, therefore, leads us to suppose that the king was originally regarded as a descendant of the sun; and this explains, I think, the etymological meaning of the word *chakravartin* used in the case of universal monarchs. The Brahmanical, Buddhist and Jaina works are unanimous in saying that preceded by the miraculous *chakra* a supreme ruler sets out on his expedition of conquest and subjects all petty princes.[2] What can this *chakra* be? This question has very much exercised scholars and antiquarians. But I cannot help thinking that this *chakra* must be the *chakra* of Vishṇu, who according to old Hindu notion, abides in him in part and whose discus alone can legitimately be supposed as affording safety to him against all his enemies. This no doubt reminds us of the Pharaohs of of Egypt who were styled *Si-re* or sons of the Sun-god and who in sculptures are represented as being protected by the rays emanating from the orb of the sun. It is quite possible that in the Brāhmaṇa period the *chakra* of Vishṇu which granted protection and safety to the kings, was really the orb of the sun darting its rays to them.

---

[1] XII. 3.5.1,

[2] See *Encyclopaedia of Religion and Ethics* under the word *Chakravartin*.

The question is here sure to be asked: Were there any checks to the arbitrariness of a king? Those who held the Social Contract theory would be the last persons to condone the misuse of authority by a king. Even such a retired and self-contained Buddhist monk as Āryadeva can scarcely keep his mind unperturbed when he sees the haughtiness of a ruler caused by his ruling power and cannot help blurting out: *Gaṇa-dāsasya te darpaḥ shaḍ-bhāgena bhṛitasya kaḥ*:[1] "What superciliousness is thine, (O king!), who art a (mere) servant of the body politic and who receivest the sixth part (of the produce) as thine wages?" Even those who held the theory of the divine origin of kingship could not have defended or tolerated the misrule and oppression of any king. A theory similar to this, is the theory of the Divine Right of Kings which was started and developed in Europe by the Christian Apostles and Fathers. We know to what absurd and pernicious extent it was carried in Europe. One of the Fathers, Irenœus *e.g.*, holds that the ruler is not only the minister of God's remedy for sin but the instrument of his punishment.[2] Much the same view was propounded by Fathers St. Ambrosiaster and St. Augustine. It was therefore no wonder at all if in his speech to Parliament in 1689

[1] V. 77.

[2] *A History of Mediæval Political Theory in the West*, Vol. I. by A. J. Carlyle, p. 148 and ff.

James II of England declared: "Kings are justly called gods; for they exercise a manner of resemblance of Divine power on earth. For if you will consider the attributes of God, you shall see how they agree in the person of a king. God hath power to create or destroy, make or unmake at his pleasure, to give life or send death, to judge all and to be accountable to none. And the like power have kings. They make and unmake their subjects; they have power of raising up and casting down; of life and death; judges over all their subjects and in all cases, yet accountable to none but God. They have power to exalt low things and abase high things and to make of their subjects like men at chess." Surely enormity cannot farther go. Fortunately for India though the divine origin of kings was maintained by some people, it was never pushed to this absurd extreme or, for the matter of that, to any absurd extent. On the contrary, even such a late work as the *Śukra-nīti*[1] says: "The king, who is virtuous, is a part of the gods. He who is otherwise is a part of the demons." It will be seen therefore that a king is a *nar·-deva* only so long as he is virtuous and that he ceases to be so the moment he goes to the bad. The theory of the divine origin of kings was thus maintained and kept within sober bounds. The Arthaśāstrakāras of India, therefore, nowhere

[1] I. 70.

show even the least inclination to defend any misconduct and repression on the part of a king. On the contrary, they are never wearied of impressing on his mind the paramount necessity of controlling passions, such as *kāma*, *krodha*, *lobha* and so forth which are called the *Śatru-shaḍ-varga* or the six enemies of the king.[1] Instances are cited of the rulers who have brought destruction upon themselves, their families and their kingdoms by falling a prey to one or another of these passions. Those who have read Kauṭilya's Arthaśāstra need not be told what I mean.[2] But perhaps it may here be said that the instances Kauṭilya has adduced are all from the Mahābhārata and the Purāṇas and have no bearing on real political life. Is there anything in his book in this connection which relates to actual practice or experience? I may therefore draw your attention to another part of his book where he starts the question: which enemy should be marched against, an enemy strong but of wicked character or an enemy weak but of righteous character? And he answers it by saying that the former should by all means be attacked, for though he is strong, his subjects will not help him but on the contrary will either put him down or go over to the other

---

[1] *Kauṭilīya*, pp. 11-2.

[2] Instances of people having killed their kings are also found in the Buddhist Jātakas, *e.g.*, *Jāt.* nos. 73 and 432.

side. And in support of his position Kauṭilya cites many verses from previous authors, one of which distinctly tells us that "when a people are impoverished, they become greedy; when they are greedy, they become disaffected; when they are disaffected, they voluntarily go to the side of the enemy or destroy their own master."[1] We cannot, therefore, help inferring that in India in the old period at any rate if the subjects were maltreated by a king, they took revenge by joining the enemy's side if he ever invaded, otherwise by actually putting their king to death. Surely historical instances of wicked and oppressive rulers being deserted or even killed by their subjects must have remained within the living memory of Kauṭilya and his predecessors, otherwise these verses would not have been composed or quoted. And we hear an echo of it even from the Mahābhārata where in at least one place we are told that "the subjects should arm themselves for slaying that king who does not protect them, who simply plunders their wealth,......and who is regarded as the most sinful of kings. That king who tells his people that he is their protector but who does not or is unable to protect them, should be slain by his combined subjects like a dog that is effected by the rabies and has

[1] *Kauṭilīya*, p. 275; also verse beginning with *tatas=sa dushṭa-prakṛitiḥ* on p. 257.

become mad[1]." Evidently, therefore, there must have been actual instances of pernicious and sinful rulers being put to death by their subjects. And all these instances must certainly have acted as a powerful deterrent to a king from giving a loose rein to his passions.

But it may be argued that the above considerations at best show that the misrule of an autocrat when it went up to an excess was put down by the people of ancient India, but that they do not necessarily show that the administration of the country was so framed that it did not allow a king to become despotic and uncontrolled. Can we say that the king's power was not arbitrary but was restrained by organisations of an opposite character? Now, it is true that in the period we have selected the regal power had considerably augmented as compared to that of the previous periods, but I confess that it could not have become arbitrary. India was then a home of self-governing communities as it continues to be to this day though now to a very limited extent. India was then studded with village, town and provincial corporations which exercised a kind of autonomy in their own spheres and managed their affairs independently or semi-independently of

---

[1] *Anuśāsana-P.*, 61.32-3; also *Śānti-P.*, 92.9, which attributes a similar doctrine to the sage Vāmadeva.

the king.[1] A similar organisation of this period was the trade and craft guilds which then flourished in numbers and were so powerful as to keep their own armies and sometimes even lend them to the king. The king was thus in those days surrounded by these tiny but numerous self-governing bodies, with their particularistic jurisdictions, which circumscribed his power. Certainly he could not afford to ignore their existence and is therefore exhorted by all Hindu epics and law-givers to respect their codes of laws and regulations and consult them. The administration of our period must, therefore, have been a system of mutual checks, and could not have left much scope for the development of the king's arbitrariness. Nay, I go a step further and say that the kings of this period themselves knew that there were great limitations to their power. A typical instance is furnished by the Telapatta-Jātaka. Here we are introduced to a king of Takshaśilā, who is enamoured of a Yakshiṇī or Ogress that has transformed herself into the most beautiful woman. Fully conscious that she had obtained a perfect mastery over the king's mind, she asks him to give her authority over his whole kingdom But what reply does the king give though he was

[1] I may have to say something of these institutions next year, but even in this lecture I have shown a little farther on how the town and provincial communities had to be consulted by a king even in regard to his succession.

hopelessly smitten with her unspeakable charms? Does he hand over the kingdom as she bids him to do? Far from it; on the contrary, he replies: "**My love, I have no power over the subjects of my kingdom; I am not their lord and master**. I have only jurisdiction over those who revolt or do wrong. So I cannot give you power and authority over the whole kingdom." But power he had over his palace, and that he gave to her. Here then we have got a king who in distinct and unmistakable words had to confess to his sweetheart that he possessed and wielded no power or authority over his state and that what little power he had was restricted to the punishment of the rebellious or the iniquitous people. A clearer limitation of the kingly power is not possible. The king could not possibly have been invested with uncontrolled and unlimited powers, at least during the period we have selected. Nay, we may proceed a step further and turn to another Jātaka story, the Eka-paṇṇa-Jātaka as it is called. Here we hear of a king's son being fierce and passionate and being called Dushṭa-kumāra for that reason. He was handed over to an ascetic for being tamed. The ascetic took the prince to a Nimb plant on which only two leaves had grown and asked him to taste one. The prince did so, but spat it out with an oath to get the taste out of his mouth. He exclaimed: "Sir, to-day the plant only suggests a deadly poison; but if left to grow, it will prove the death of many persons;" and forthwith he plucked up and crushed the tiny growth. Thereupon the ascetic said: "Prince, dreading what the poisonous seedling might grow to, you have torn it up and rent it asunder. Even as you acted to the tree, so the people of this kingdom, dreading what a prince so fierce and passionate, may become when king, will not place you on the throne but uproot you like this Nimb plant and drive you forth to exile." It is quite clear that the people not only exercised control over the king's power but also could prevent his son from succeeding to his throne if necessary. An instance of this kind has been mentioned in the Uddyoga-Parvan of the Mahābhārata also. A king called Pratīpa, having become exceedingly aged, made preparations for crowning his eldest and favourite son Devāpi. The latter was no doubt possessed of many virtues, but had contracted a skin-disease, and was, therefore, unfit in the popular opinion to hold the reins of government. The subjects—the Brāhmaṇs and the Town (*paura*) and Country (*jānapada*) people—therefore objected. The king burst into tears but had to yield to the popular voice.[1] In the Rāmāyaṇa also we find

[1] 148. 21-7. Sagara also is said to have exiled his eldest son Asamañjas at the desire of the people because he used to drown their children in the river Sarayū (*Śānti*-P., 579). Khanīnetra is also said to have been deposed by his subjects, and his son installed in his place (*Aśvamedha*—P., 4. 8-9).

that Daśaratha consecrated his son Rāma as crown-prince only after respectfully securing the consent of the Brāhmaṇs, generals (*bala-mukhya*) and the Town (*paura*) and Country (*jānapada*) people[1].

I have told you before (p. 123) that both the Artha—and the Dharma-śāstra ordain that a king shall make good out of his own treasury any property of his subject that has been robbed by thieves but cannot be recovered. It is worthy of note that there is thus a perfect agreement on this point between the Artha-śāstra and the Dharma-śāstra. And certainly they both would not have laid down the law in this manner if such had not been the practice. And this certainly would not have been the practice if the popular voice had not been strong enough to enforce it. So even for such a trifling matter as the stolen property of a private individual the king was controlled by the people! The royal power could not possibly have been absolute, at any rate, in the period we have selected.

There was yet another check to the arbitrariness of a king which we have to notice here. There was placed before him not only the selfish point of view which advised him not to run up to an extreme and cause disaffection among his people but also a higher and spiritual

---

[1] II. 2, 15 and ff. Yayāti similarly crowned his youngest son, king only after satisfying the people who strongly protested because they at first thought that the eldest prince was being unnecessarily set aside.

point of view which, I think, was no less efficacious. In Chapter 75 of the Śānti-Parvan we are told that a king attains a fourth part of the spiritual merit or sin that his subjects commit. The same idea we find better explained in the Uddyoga-Parvan. Here however only one-sixth part of the virtue or sin of the subjects is said to accrue to the king. And the question is started whether any particular Age makes a king what he is or whether it is the king who makes the Age what it is. The question is answered by saying: *rājā kālasya kāraṇam*, *i.e.* it is really the king who makes the Age what it is. If he is virtuous and enforces the Daṇḍa-nīti or the science of government in its entirety and in the proper spirit, he will inaugurate the Kṛita Age. But if he is all sinful, the Kali Age must set in. It is thus the king who is held responsible for good or bad government and for making his people virtuous or otherwise. And a belief is expressed that one-fourth or one-sixth part of the merit or sin of his subjects must perforce go to him.[1] In these days when scepticism is rampant and no certitude is felt about the future world, such an expression of the reward and punishment to a king is apt to be looked upon as devoid of any force or meaning. But in ancient times when the spiritual was felt to

---

[1] *Uddyoga-P.*, 131, 12 & ff.; this curious doctrine has been set forth also in *Śānti-P.*, 69. 79 & ff.; and in *Anuśāsana-P.*, 61.34 & 36.

be more real than the temporal, it is not difficult to imagine how powerful and effective this belief must have been in both stimulating him to good government and deterring him from misconduct and misrule.

LECTURE—IV.

ADMINISTRATIVE HISTORY (*Contd.*).

Saṁgha Form of Political Government.

In my last lecture I referred to the monarchical form of Government and the various notions prevalent in regard to the origin and nature of kingship. I then told you that there was also another form of Government called Saṁgha or Gaṇa. Let us now see what its characteristic features were. Before, however I discuss this question, it is necessary to state that it was Prof. Rhys Davids who first pointed out that this form of Government was flourishing side by side with monarchy in North India about the time of the rise of Buddhism. It was afterwards Mr. K. P. Jayaswal, who perceived the importance of this subject and brought it to the more prominent notice of the students of ancient Indian history. In the article he has published[1] he has collected much information bearing upon it, from which it is possible to draw a number of interesting conclusions. It is a pity that no scholar has so far come forward to further advance our knowledge of the question. This task, therefore, I set to myself in

[1] *Modern Review*, 1913, pp. 585-41 and 664-68.

the present lecture, which, it will be seen, presents the subject in a somewhat different light.

Most of you will perhaps wonder what the word Saṁgha and Gaṇa could mean and how in particular they could denote any non-monarchical form of Government, or Government of the many as I have told you before. The words mean a corporate collection, an aggregation of individuals for a definite purpose. The terms were certainly known to Pāṇini, and were thus current about the middle of the 7th century B. C. to which period he has to be assigned. They occur in no less than three of his Sūtras. One of these is *Saṁgh-odghau gaṇa-praśaṁsayoḥ*[1]. This Sūtra is very important, but unfortunately its proper meaning has not been perceived. The word *saṁgha* comes from the root *saṁ + han*, "to collect, to gather." The regular noun form from it is *saṁghāta*, which means merely 'a collection or assemblage.' But there is another noun derived from it, though it is irregularly formed, *viz.* *saṁgha*. Pāṇini is, therefore, compelled to make a special *sūtra* to acknowledge its existence in

[1] III. 3. 86; the second Sūtra is III. 3. 42, which teaches the formation of the word *nikāya* in the sense of 'a Saṁgha but without any conception of its gradation.' The third is V. 2. 52. From the time of Buddha onwards we find the word *Gaṇa* used to denote religious and political bodies. In the former case it was employed promiscuously with *Saṁgha*. But in the political sense, *Gaṇa* denoted only one kind of Saṁgha, *viz.* an oligarchy, as we shall see subsequently.

the spoken language and to tell us that it does not signify a mere collection as the other word, *viz. saṁghāta*, does, but, a *gaṇa*, *i.e.* a special kind of collection, or a corporate collection as I have just said. It will thus be seen that the technical senses of these words were known to Pāṇini.

Saṁgha or Gaṇa is, therefore, not a promiscuous conglomeration, but a combination of individuals for a definite object, in other words, a corporate body. It will be seen that there can be as many kinds of Saṁghas as there are different purposes with which they can be constituted. And, as a matter of fact, it was so in ancient India, and especially in the period with which we are dealing. If we have a fraternity composed of persons devoted to a particular set of religious beliefs, we have a religious Saṁgha, the most typical example of which is the Buddhist Saṁgha. It is a mistake to suppose that Buddha was the first religious founder to appropriate the term Saṁgha to the brotherhood originated by him. The Pāli Canon itself mentions no less than seven religious teachers like Buddha who were his contemporaries, *viz.* Pūraṇa-Kassapa, Makkhali-Gosāla, and so forth. These have all been called *Saṁghino*, heads of Saṁghas, *Gaṇino*, heads of Gaṇas and *Gaṇāchariyā*, teachers of Gaṇas.[1] It will thus be perceived that the brotherhood founded by Buddha was

[1] *E.g.* the *Mahā-parinibbāna-sutta*, 58.

not the only religious order known as Saṁgha but even in his time there were no less than seven which were similary styled Saṁgha or Gaṇa. Nay, these heads of religious Saṁghas are said to have been Samaṇa-brāhmaṇā,[1] which means that while some of these Saṁghas were Śramaṇa, others were Brahmanical, orders. This clearly shows that there were sects of Brahmanical ascetics also which were designated Saṁghas or Gaṇas.[2] Saṁgha, as a word for 'a religious order', was common both to the Brahmanical and non-Brahmanical sects.

So much for the Saṁgha or body formed for a religious purpose. But we may also have a Saṁgha for the purpose of trade and industry or, in other words, a trade or craft guild. You will be surprised if I tell you that from about 500 B. C. to 600 A. D. India was studded with craft guilds of various types showing how well industry and trade were specialised and developed.

---

[1] In translating the passage from this *sutta*, Prof. Rhys Davids missed the true sense of the terms *Saṁgha* and *Gaṇa* and also of the phrase Samaṇa-brāhmaṇa (SBE., XI. 105 and n. 1). The latter he translates by "the Brahmans by saintliness of life" and not by "Samaṇas and Brāhmaṇs," because none of the heads of these religious Saṁghas was a Brāhmaṇ according to the *Sumaṅgala-vilāsinī*. How far the authority of this commentary in this matter is reliable I do not know, but that the phrase *samaṇa-brāhmaṇa* is a Dvandva and not a Karmadhāraya compound as Prof. Rhys Davids takes it, is clear from the following: *Nāhaṇ-taṁ passāmi samaṇaṁ vā brāhmaṇaṁ vā saṅghiṁ gaṇiṁ gaṇāchariyaṁ*, etc. (*Maj-N.*, I. 227).

[2] Compare *e.g.* the phrase *pañchannaṁ isi-satānaṁ Gaṇa-satthā* which we meet with in the Jātakas (II. 41. 10-11; 72. 12 and &c.).

This is not the place to give an account of these guilds or Śreṇis as they were technically called. These I hope to describe in one of my lectures some year. What I here want to say is that the Śreṇis were really Saṁghas and have been so called by Kauṭilya in his Artha-śāstra.[1] Kauṭilya distinguishes between three kinds of Saṁghas, one of which is *vārt-opajīvin*, *i.e.* dependent upon industry, and is also styled Śreṇin by him.

A third class of Saṁgha is *āyudha-jīvin* as Pāṇini calls it, or *śastr-opajīvin* as Kauṭilya styles it, both expressions meaning '(a corporation) subsisting on arms.' This Saṁgha as a rule, denoted tribal bands of mercenaries, and constituted one kind of the king's army.[2] Pāṇini mentions several of them, some situated in Vāhīka and some in Trigarta, both parts of the Panjāb. But perhaps the most interesting, referred to by him are the Yaudheyas, Parśus, Asuras and Rakshases. Of the Yaudheyas

---

[1] The expression actually used here is *Kāmbhoja-Surāshṭra-kshatriya-śreṇy-ādayo vārtā-śastr-opajīvinaḥ* (p. 376), which I render as follows: "Kambhoja and Surāshṭra *śreṇis* (guilds), Kshatriya *śreṇis* (fighting corporations) and so forth are (Saṁghas) which subsist on industry and arms." Elsewhere too Kauṭilya distinguishes *śreṇi* (guild) from an *āyudhīya* (fighting) body (p. 263).

[2] When I say that these Saṁghas were tribal bands of mercenaries, I do not mean that any particular band of them must necessarily exhaust the whole tribe. This certainly was not the case with the Yaudheyas as we shall see later on. Though in Kauṭilya's time the fighting Saṁghas were Kshatriyas, in Pāṇini's time some of them were also Brāhmaṇs, as is no doubt implied from his Sūtra, V. 3, 114.

I shall speak later on. Parśus are certainly the Persis, or old Persians, and Asuras the Assyrians.[1] Rakshases must be the same as Rākshasas, an aboriginal race referred to in early Sanskrit works, and in particular the Rāmāyaṇa. This indicates that some of the mercenary bands at any rate were foreigners. What the exact constitution of this Saṁgha was is far from clear. But as these fighting bands have all been called Saṁgha, there must have been some code of rules according to which they were formed and continued their existence. At any rate, a *Yodhājīva* or mercenary soldier, who was a *gāmaṇi*, is mentioned in the Saṁyutta-Nikāya[2] as discoursing with Buddha. As the word *gāmaṇi, i.e. grāmaṇī* shows, he must have been the head of a fighting Saṁgha. From his talk with Buddha it seems that there were many old Āchāryas among them who themselves were soldiers and who held out to those dying on the battle-field the hope of becoming one with Sarañjita gods.

There are two or three other classes of Saṁghas which have been referred to in

---

[1] That most of the allusions to the Asuras in the Śatapatha-Brāhmaṇa refer to a foreign tribe has been clearly established by Mr. Jayaswal in a note which he contributed to the ZDMG. immediately before the war and the rough copy of which he was kind enough to show me. This emboldens me in identifying the Asuras with the Assyrians and consequently the Parśus with the Persis.

[2] IV. 308-9.

the Buddhist and Brahmanical literature, but there is no need of mentioning them here, as the instances I have already given are enough to show what a Saṁgha or Gaṇa really signifies. A Saṁgha is a corporate body of individuals formed for a definite purpose. Let us now turn to the political Saṁgha, which, as I have already told you, denotes the rule of the many, and which again was of three or four different kinds. It is really difficult to translate this Saṁgha by any single English word, but the term 'republic' as understood in old Greek political philosophy, makes the nearest approach to it. What is to be remembered is that this Saṁgha possessed not Sovereign One but Sovereign Number. At this stage it is necessary to inform you that ordinarily the words *saṁgha* and *gaṇa* are used synonymously, but that the term *gaṇa* is also used in a specific sense, *viz.* to denote a particular kind of political Saṁgha. But I may be asked to state here, at the outset, what authority at all I have for saying that there were political Saṁghas. Now, the *Āyāraṁga-Sutta*,[1] a well-known Jaina Canonical work, lays down certain rules in regard to the tours of the Jaina monks and nuns and tells us in one place what countries they are not to visit. The countries that are so tabooed are *a-rāya* (*i.e.* where there is no

---

[1] (P.T.S.), II. 3. 1. § 10.

ruler), *juva-rāya* (where the ruler is a youngster), *do-rajja* (government by two), and also *gaṇa-rāya* (*i.e.* where Gaṇa is the ruling authority). As all the states which the Jaina Brotherhood is ordained to avoid are unquestionably of a political nature, no reasonable doubt can be entertained as to this Gaṇa being a political Gaṇa. Another authority also can be cited, though it is of a somewhat later period. A work of the Northern Buddhists called the Avadāna-Śataka (Circa 100 B.C.) speaks in its *avadāna* No. 88 of certain merchants as having gone from the Madhya-déśa or Middle Country to the Dekkan. And there we are told that when they were asked as to how their country was governed, they replied by saying that *kechid=deśā Gaṇ-ādhīnāḥ kechid=rāj-ādhīnā iti* "some territories are subject to Gaṇas and some to Kings." Evidently Gaṇa is here contrasted with Rājan, and as the latter represents 'the political rule of One' the former must be taken to represent 'the political rule of Many.' Again, Pāṇini gives a Sūtra, *viz. janapada-śabdāt Kshatri-yād=añ*[1], which means that the affix *añ* comes in the sense of a descendant after a word which, while denoting a country, expresses also a Kshatriya tribe or clan. To this Kātyāyana adds a *vārtika, viz. Kshatriyād=eka-rājāt Saṁgha-pratishedhārtham.* It is true, as Pāṇini says,

[1] IV. 1. 168.

that the affix is to be applied to a word *e.g.* Pañchāla which denotes both a Kshatriya tribe and the country inhabited by them. But Kātyāyana says that this Kshatriya tribe must be *eka-rāja, i.e.* possessed of Individual Sovereign in order to exclude a Kshatriya tribe which is a Saṁgha, *i.e.* a Kshatriya tribe which has Collegiate Sovereign. This exactly agrees with what Kauṭilya tells us. I have just told you that he distinguishes between three kinds of Saṁghas, one of which is *vārt-opajīvin* or a craft guild and another *śastr-opajīvin* or a mercenary tribal band. The third Saṁgha, he says, is *rāja-śabd-opajīvin, i.e.* an organisation all the members of which bear the title *rājan*[1]. In my last lecture I informed you that the Lichchhavis and the Mallas were typical examples of this Saṁgha. These tribes have been constantly mentioned in the Buddhist Pāli Canon. And the Majjhima-Nikāya in one place distinctly calls them Saṁgha and Gaṇa[2]. We were introduced here to a discussion between Buddha and a Jaina monk called Sachchaka. In the course of the discussion the former asked whether Pasenadi, king of Kosala, or Ajātśatru, king of Magadha, had power to banish, burn,

---

[1] *Arthaśāstra*, 376.

[2] I. 231; I do not think that the words *saṁgha* and *gaṇa* are here used exactly synonymously. Saṁgha here is the genus and Gaṇa a species. The Lichchhavis and Mallas were specifically Gaṇas.

or kill a man in his dominions. At the time of this discussion, some Lichchhavis were present. And by pointing to them Sachchaka answers Buddha, saying that if the Saṁghas and Gaṇas, like the Lichchhavis or the Mallas, had this power in their own *vijita* or kingdom, certainly Pasenadi and Ajātaśatru did possess it. This indicates that the Lichchhavis and the Mallas were Saṁghas or Gaṇas and had their own territory where their power was supreme. It is thus clear that Saṁgha denotes 'a rule by numbers'.

The best known form of political Saṁgha is Gaṇa. What I have said so far to prove the existence of the political Saṁgha applies really to Gaṇa. This Gaṇa, as Kātyāyana and Kauṭilya give us to understand, was tribal in character and was confined to the Kshatriya order. It is a pity that no account of its internal constitution has been given in the Arthaśāstras, where we might naturally expect it. Under such circumstances the Buddhist Pāli works and Chapter 107 of the Śāntiparvan of the Mahābhārata are our only source of information. Very little do we know even from this source, but we have to be content even with that little. We have seen that the capital of the Lichchhavis was Vesāli. The preambles of the Jātakas[1] or Buddha's Birth-stories tell us

---

[1] III. 1; IV. 148.

in two places that there were 7707 Lichchhavi kings staying in Vesāli to administer the affairs of the State. This agrees with the statement of Kauṭilya, quoted above, that the members of the Saṁgha were all designated kings. Quite in keeping with this we find the sons of these Lichchhavi kings called Lichchhavi-kumāras or Lichchhavi princes. As kings they were also entitled to coronation. We hear of there having been a special *pushkariṇī* or tank in Vesāli, the water of which was used to sprinkle their heads while being crowned. The tank was considered very sacred, and was, therefore, covered with an iron net so that not even a bird could get through, and a strong guard was set to prevent any one taking water from it[1]. It is not, however, clear whether these Lichchhavi kings were crowned all at one time, and, if so, on what occasions. As every one of the Lichchhavi Saṁgha was a king, the probability is that on the death of any one of them his son who succeeded to his title and property was alone crowned king.

The actual wording used in connection with the sacred tank which supplied water for coronation is *Vesāli-nagare Gaṇa-rājakulānaṁ abhiseka-maṅgala-pokkharaṇi etc.*[2]. Here the phrase *Gaṇa-rājakula* is important. It shows that the

---

[1] *Jāt.* IV. 148-9.

[2] Ibid, IV. 148: ll. 21-2.

political Saṁgha called Gaṇa was composed of various *rājakulas* or royal families, and that the heads of these *rājakulas* constituted the Gaṇa. This receives confirmation also from Kātyāyana, the author of a Smṛiti, who says that *kulānāṁ tu samūhas=tu Gaṇaḥ sa parikīrtitaḥ,*[1] *i.e.* a Gaṇa (whether political or otherwise) is an aggregation of families. The account of the political Saṁgha given by Kauṭilya also shows that it consisted of Kulas or families. This is also clear from Chapter 107 of the Śāntiparvan referred to above. The members of a Gaṇa are there said to be *jātyā cha sadṛiśāḥ sarve kulena sadṛiśās=tathā, i.e.* exact equals of one another in respect of birth and family, and it is expressly stated that if quarrels break out amongst the Kulas, the Elders of the Kulas should by no means remain indifferent, otherwise the Gaṇa will be dissolved.[2] The political Saṁgha designated Gaṇa thus presupposes the existence of manifold royal families or clans, and consisted of their heads who were styled kings. But even in a republic of the present day where the ideas of liberty, equality and fraternity are being imbibed and assimilated, the executive function has remained only to the select few. Such was also the case with the political Saṁgha of Ancient

---

[1] *Parāśara-Mādhava* (Bib. Ind.), III, 250.

[2] Vs. 27, 28 and 30.

India. We not unfrequently hear of Saṁgha-mukhyas and Gaṇa-mukhyas. They are mentioned not only by Kauṭilya[1] but also in the Śāntiparvan. I quote three verses from the latter bearing on the point:

Tasmān=mānayitavyās=te
Gaṇa-mukhyāḥ pradhānataḥ
loka-yātrā samāyattā
bhūyasī teshu pārthiva
Mantra-guptiḥ pradhāneshu
chāraś=ch=āmitra-karshaṇa
na Gaṇāḥ kritsnaśo mantraṁ
śrotum=arhanti Bhārata
Gaṇa-mukhyais=tu sambhūya
kāryaṁ Gaṇa-hitaṁ mithaḥ

—Chap. 107, vs. 23-25.

TRANSLATION.

"Hence they that are the Chiefs of the Gaṇa should be especially honoured. The affairs of the kingdom, O King, depend to a great extent upon them.

"The safeguarding of the (secret) State counsels and espionage, O crusher of foes, should remain with the Chiefs only.

"It is not advisable that any Gaṇa, as a whole, should know the (secret) counsels, O Bhārata.

"But the Chiefs of a Gaṇa, having assembled in secret, should do what is for the good of the Gaṇa."

[1] *Arthaśāstra*, 377.

It is clear from the above passage that a select few were appointed by a Gaṇa from among themselves. They constituted what may be called a Cabinet, and were in charge of the Department of espionage and also of all State affairs of a highly important and confidential character. This agrees with what Bṛihaspati, the author of a Smṛiti, lays down. The verses from his work are:

Sarva-kārye pravīṇāś=cha kartavyāś=cha mahattamāḥ II dvau trayaḥ pañcha vā kāryāḥ samūha-hita-vādinaḥ I kartavyaṁ vachanaṁ teshāṁ grāma-śreṇi-Gaṇ-ādibhiḥ II.[1]

What these verses tell us is that two, three or five members of a corporate body should be appointed as Mahattamas or Chiefs and their counsels should be carried out by a Gaṇa, craft-guild or village community.

It will be seen from what I have cited that the real executive lay in the hands of the Gaṇa-Mukhyas, who again were not one but many; in other words, power was not centred in one single individual. No single member of the Gaṇa was thus by himself a ruler or Rājan in the proper sense of the term. And this is the reason why Kauṭilya styles them *Rāja-śabdin*, which means that they were Rājans in name. This receives support from the Lalita-vistara[2]

[1] *Vivādaratnākara*, 179.

[2] Lefmann's Ed., p. 21.

which says about the Lichchhavis that *ekaika=eva manyate ahaṁ rājā ahaṁ rāj=eti*, *i.e.* "every one thinks: 'I am king, I am king,'" when none of them singly was.

I have told you before that the preambles of two Jātakas inform us that there were 7707 Lichchhavi kings in Vesāli, the capital of their dominions. One Jātaka further informs us that there were as many Uparājas or viceroys, Senāpatis or generals and Bhāṇḍāgārikas or treasurers staying with the kings at Vesāli. It appears that every one of these Lichchhavi kings had with him his own viceroy, general and treasurer. The Aṭṭhakathā and Sumaṅgalavilāsinī, which are commentaries on the Buddhist Pāli Canon works, afford us some interesting glimpses into the manner in which Law was administered by the Lichchhavis or the Vajjīs as they are also called.[1] It is true that these commentaries were written about the fifth century A.D., but as they are known to have preserved many interesting historical details of the period when Buddha lived and preached, their account of the judicial adminstration of the Vajjian kingdom is certainly worth considering. When a culprit was found, we are told, he was in the first instance sent to an officer called Viniśchaya-Mahāmātra.

[1] JRAS., VII. 993. n. 2; *Kachchāyana's Pāli Grammar* by James D' Alwis, 99-100.

If he was found guilty, he was transferred to the Vyavahārika, then to the Sūtradhara (rehearser of law-maxim), Ashṭa-kulika (officer appointed over eight *kulas*[1]), Senāpati (general), Uparāja (viceroy), and finally to Rājan (king). The Rājan consulted the *Paveṇi-potthaka* or "Book of Precedents," and inflicted a suitable punishment.

Whether there were as many as 7707 Lichchhavi kings ever staying in Vesāli, as the Jātaka preambles inform us, is somewhat doubtful. What we may safely infer is that the number of the kings constituting the Lichchhavi Gaṇa was pretty large. It again seems that the Lichchhavi kings had each his separate principality where he exercised supreme power in certain respects. Except on this supposition it is not intelligible why each should have his own Uparāja, Senāpati and Bhāṇḍāgārika, and act as the magistrate in inflicting punishments. Nevertheless, the Gaṇa as a whole had power to kill, burn or exile a man from their *vijita* or kingdom which meant the aggregate of the principalities of the different kings, as the passage referred to above from the Majjhima-nikāya clearly indicates. The Lichchhavi kings, again, appear to be in the habit of

[1] The expression occurs also in one of the Dāmodarpur grants which are being edited by Prof. Radhagovinda Basak. As regards *kula* see *Manu*, VII. 119.

staying not in their petty States but in the capital town, Vesāli, and along with their superior officers, *viz.* Uparāja, Senāpati and Bhāṇḍāgārika, leaving in their respective principalities their subordinate staff, such as the Viniśchaya-Mahāmātra, Vyavahārika and so forth. In what matters individually in the several states and in what matters conjointly in the whole kingdom the Lichchhavi kings exercised autonomy is not clear. This, however, is certain that their Saṁgha was a federation of the heads of some of the clans constituting the tribe.

The most typical examples of this political Saṁgha, as I have said, are the Lichchhavis or Vajjīs and the Mallas. In my second lecture I have said that the former held Videha and parts of Kosala and had their capital at Vesāli which has been identified with Basaṛh in the Muzaffarpur District of Bihār. The capital of the Mallas was Kusinārā or Kasiā. Both these tribes have been mentioned by Kauṭilya, but he specifies four others which were similarly *Rāja-śabd-opajīvi* Saṁghas. These four are Madrakas, Kukuras, Kurus and Pañchālas.[1] The Madrakas occupied the country between the Rāvī and the Chenāb in the Panjāb.[2] What province the Kukuras had occupied is not certain,

[1] *Arthaśāstra*, 376.

[2] JRAS., 1897, 839.

but most probably they were settled in North Gujarāt.[1] The capital of the Kurus was Indraprastha near Delhi, and of the Pañchālas, Kāmpilya identified with Kāmpil between Budaon and Farrukhabad in U. P.[2] In another place in his Arthaśāstra, Kauṭilya speaks of the Vṛishṇi Saṁgha also. We have independent evidence also to attest the existence of the Vṛishṇi Saṁgha. At least two coins are known, the legends of which, as clearly read by Mr. A. V. Bergny for the first time, show that they belonged to the Vṛishṇi Gaṇa.[3] No doubt need, therefore, be entertained as to the Vṛishṇis being a Gaṇa. There certainly must have been many other tribes which were Gaṇas. Some of these have been noticed by foreign writers along with other Saṁghas. The foreign writers, whose statements can be of any use to us for the period we have selected, must of course be the Greeks who wrote accounts of Alexander's invasion of India. Let us see whether they make any mention of Saṁghas, and if so, what remarks they offer in regard to their constitution. One tribe in the Panjāb, which was settled on the lower Akesines

---

1 Kukura is twice associated with Aparānta, once in the Nāsik Cave inscription of Vāsishṭhīputra Puḷumāvi and another time in the Junāgaḍh rock inscription of Rudradāman (EI., VIII. 44 and 60). As Aparānta is Konkan, Kukura should correspond to Gujarāt.

2 Above, p. 52.

3 JRAS., 1900, 416 and 420-1.

(Chenab), is designated Abastanoi by Arrian, Sambastai by Diodorus, Sabarcae by Curtius and Sabagrae by Orosius.[1] They are identified with the Ambashṭhas of the Mahābhārata by some[2] and with the Śaubhreyas grouped along with the Yaudheyas in the Yaudheya-gaṇa of Pāṇini by others.[3] In regard to this people Curtius says that "they were a powerful Indian tribe where the form of government was democratic and not regal." According to Diodorus "they were a people inferior to none in India either for numbers or for bravery and they dwelt in cities in which the democratic form of government prevailed." Arrian, again, mentions three tribes, Kathanians, Oxydrakai and Malloi, which he describes as independent republics.[4] And in respect of the Malloi, in particular, Arrian tells us that when they submitted to Alexander, they informed him that "they were attached more than any others to freedom and autonomy, and that their freedom they had preserved intact from the time Dionysos came to India until Alexander's invasion.[5] Oxydrakai are of course to be identified with Kshaudrakas and Malloi with Mālavas, which both have been mentioned

---

[1] Mc. Crindle's *Ancient India: Its invasion by Alexander the Great*, 155, 252 and 292.

[2] Ibid, 155, n. 2.

[3] IA., I, 23.

[4] Mc. Crindle, 115.

[5] Ibid, 154.

as Saṁgha tribes by Patañjali.[1] Two other Panjāb tribes I will note which have been noticed by Alexander's historians. When the Macedonian monarch went to Nysa, "the Nysians," says Arrian, "sent out to him their president, whose name was Akouphis and along with him thirty deputies of their most eminent citizens to entreat him to spare the city........." Alexander "confirmed the inhabitants of Nysa in the enjoyment of their freedom and their own laws : and when he enquired about their laws, he praised them because the government of their state was in the hands of the aristocracy. He moreover requested them to send with him 300 of their horsemen, together with 100 of their best men selected from the governing body, which consisted of 300 members......when Akouphis heard this, he is said to have smiled at the request, and when Alexander asked him why he laughed, to have replied, 'How, O King! can a single city if deprived of a hundred of its best men continue to be well-governed?......"[2] Now, what do we find? We have no less than five tribes and peoples mentioned as being situated in the Panjāb and Sind by the Greek and Macedonian historians of Alexander's invasion. I do not want to enter into any detailed discussion in this place, but it is enough if I say here that

[1]. His gloss on Pāṇini, IV. 1, 168.
[2] Mc. Crindle, 79-81.

as their form of government is said to be not regal but democratic or aristocratic, these tribes must be looked upon as political Saṁghas. A Greek author at least would not fall into the blunder of calling a government democratic or aristocratic if it was not really so.[1]

Our account of the political Saṁgha will not, I am afraid, be complete unless I say a few words about Kula, its corporate unit. Kula, you are aware, denotes a clan or group of families. In the Aṅguttara-Nikāya [2] we have a passage in which Buddha distinguishes between the different kinds of rulers. In the concluding portion of it we are told that one class of rulers was Pūga-gāmaṇikas or, as the commentator explains it, Gaṇa-jeṭṭhaks, *i.e.* Elders of a Gaṇa, and that another class of rulers was *Ye vā pana Kulesu pachchek-ādhipachcham kārenti*, *i.e.* those who severally exercise autonomy (*ādhipatyam*) over the Kulas or clans. Perhaps a most typical example of this kind of rule is furnished by the Śākya clan to which Buddha himself belonged. This clan had spread itself over a number of towns. The chief town, of course, was Kapilavastu. But there were other townships belonging to the Śākyas, such as Chātuma, Sāmagāma,

---

[1] Megasthenes also refers to republics in Ancient India. Thus he makes the general remark that "those who live near the sea have no kings" and also mentions the Maltecorae and four other tribes who "are free and have no kings" (I.A., VI. 340-1).

[2] III, 76.

Khomadussa, Devadaha and so forth[1]. There are no grounds to suppose that an office-holder was appointed by the Śākyas from time to time as Prof. Rhys Davids has said[2]. The Pāli Canon speaks only once of a king of the Śākyas. This king that they mention is Bhaddiya[3], and the words used are *Bhaddiyo Sakya-rājā Sakyānaṁ rajjaṁ kāreti.* The word here employed is *rājā,* who, in the period when Buddha lived, was not elected but hereditary, and was not a mere president but a ruler. If Bhaddiya had really been a periodic office-holder, he would have been designated not Rājā, but Mukhya or Grāmaṇī. We must not suppose that the king of the Śākyas was merely the chief of a clan, and had no sovereignty over any people outside his clan. In the villages and towns held by the Śākyas, there were, besides the Śākyas, artisans and men of special higher trades such as the carpenters, smiths and potters who had villages of their own. There were Brāhmaṇs also whose services were

---

[1] Rhys Davids' *Buddhist India*, 18.

[2] Ibid, 19.

[3] VP., II, 181. The preambles of some Jātakas (*e.g.* Nos. 466 and 536) lead us to infer that the Śākyas were a Gaṇa and not a Kula. But these preambles do not form part of the Buddhist Canon and are certainly of a much later age than the Vinaya-Piṭaka. What is narrated by them is based not upon contemporary or very nearly contemporary evidence, but rather upon traditions handed down by *Āchāryas,* which were sometimes conflicting or different (*e.g. Jāt.,* V. 413. 10). The Jātaka preambles cannot, therefore, be taken as possessing any authority when they run counter to what the canonical texts say.

requisitioned at every domestic event and who had their settlements in the Śākya country[1]. The Śākya chief was, therefore, not only the chief of his clan but was a veritable ruler or Rājā. This is also proved by the fact that Bhaddiya speaks of his being protected by a body guard wherever he went and also of his Nagara and Janapada—the capital town and kingdom—exactly the terms technical to the political administration. This is the *Kulādhipatya* alluded to by Buddha which denotes not merely chiefship of a clan but also sovereignty over the territory occupied by the clan.

Let us now pause here for a while and try to digest the mass of information we have collected about the political Saṁgha. One kind of this Saṁgha, *viz.* Gaṇa, I have repeatedly told you, was a tribal organisation. But if you suppose that its sovereignty was confined merely to the tribe, nothing can be more erroneous. When a Gaṇa-Saṁgha is spoken of as having a *vijita* or kingdom and as having power to burn, kill or exile a man as we have seen above, there can be no question about sovereignty being vested in this body. The fact that there were Uparājas, Senāpatis, Bhāṇḍāgārikas and so forth connected with the Saṁgha completely confirms our conclusion, and clearly establishes its political character. The lowest political unit

1 *Buddhist India*, 20-1.

seems to be the Kula whose sovereignty is described as *Kulādhipatya*. It denotes not simply the domination of a Chief over his clan but also and principally his supremacy over the territory occupied by that clan. According to the Aryan social structure, every family (Kuṭumba) or household (Gṛiha) had its head who was designated Kuṭumbin or Gṛihapati. The group more extensive than the family was the Kula or clan which also had its head. This formation seems to have been common at least to the first three grades of the Hindu Society, the Brāhmaṇas, Kshatriyas and Vaiśyas. But then the functions of each grade had become differentiated and specialised long before the period we have selected, and we know that the duty of the Kshatriya order was primarily to rule. Two kinds of authority had the Kshatriyas therefore to exercise—one over their Kula and Gṛiha or Kuṭumba in common with the other classes of the Hindu Society and the other over the territory which they conquered and occupied as Kshatriyas. A Kshatriya Gṛihapati or Kuṭumbin we do not hear of as having ever become a ruler. It is the head of a Kshatriya Kula or clan that attains to sovereignty. The reason is not very difficult to understand. A territory that is to be ruled over has to be conquered, and for a territory to be conquered a sufficiently large band of fighting men is necessary. No members of a single Kshatriya family (Kuṭumba or Gṛiha) can ever be expected by themselves to acquire any strip of territory. It is only a Kula or clan, which, because it consists of a great many households, and consequently a large number of fighters, that can be reasonably expected to conquer any tract of land. This was the case with the Śākyas whom I have cited as an instance of Kula sovereignty. They were a clan, a branch of the Ikshvāku tribe. The province seized by them was called Śākya country after them and was governed by one ruler, and we know that it was occupied not by the Śākyas alone but also by the Brāhmaṇs, artisans and traders.

As the chief of a Kshatriya clan becomes the ruler of the country conquered and occupied by them, the sovereignty must confine itself to the family of that chief. Such a Kshatriya clan is *eka-rāja, i.e.* with Sovereign One, as Kātyāyana calls it. But we have instances of Kshatriya clans, originally of monarchical constitution, becoming aristocracies. I have already informed you that the Kurus and Pañchālas are mentioned by Kauṭilya as *rāja-śabd-opajīvi* Saṁghas. But the Jātakas and early Pāli literature clearly give us to understand that they were not Saṁgha but *eka-rāja* Kshatriya clans, *i.e.* clans each governed by one ruler. This means that in the sixth and fifth centuries before Christ, Kurus and Pañchālas were monarchical clans but became non-monarchical in the fourth century when Kauṭilya lived. We know that members of the royal family were often given a share in the administration of a country, and in proportion as this share would become less and less formal, would the state organisation lose the form of absolute monarchy and approach that of an oligarchy.[1] The chief feature of a Gaṇa, as we have seen, is its division into Kulas. In other words, the political power lay in the hands, not of the whole people but of a few families who constituted the Gaṇa. This characteristic can apply, not to a democracy but to an oligarchy into which alone a monarchy can glide when it becomes a Gaṇa. And we know that this characteristic was possessed by the political Saṁghas mentioned by Kauṭilya. We shall not, therefore, be far from right, if we consider the Kuru and Pañchāla Saṁghas as instances of the Oligarchic form of Government.

A third instance is furnished by the Yaudheyas and in a curious manner. We have already seen that they have been mentioned by Pāṇini as an *āyudha-jīvi* Saṁgha. But, on the other hand, it must be remembered that from

[1] Cf. Grote's *History of Greece*, Pt. II, Cap. IX. Sidgwick says: "But speaking broadly and generally, it is doubtless safe to affirm that when political society passed in Greece out of the stage of primitive kingship, it passed into that of primitive oligarchy."—*The Development of European Polity*, p. 72.

his Sūtra IV. 1. 178 it is clear that they were an *eka-rāja* Kshatriya tribe even in Pāṇini's time. It may seem strange how a tribe, which is once described as an *āyudha-jīvi* Saṁgha, could be said to be a monarchical tribe. But really there is no discrepancy here, because firstly, an *āyudha-jīvi* Saṁgha bears no political character at all. Secondly, such a Saṁgha need not include all the members af the tribe. We can, therefore, very well suppose that there were some Yaudheyas who did not come under this Saṁgha and that politically they were a Kshatriya tribe of the monarchical type in Pāṇini's time. But about the beginning of the Christian era at any rate they seem to have acquired the nature of a political Saṁgha. This is indicated by the issue of their coinage which ranges between 50 and 350 A.D.[1] Like the Mālavas they style themselves Gaṇa on their money. So they were a Gaṇa, a political Saṁgha, when they struck these coins. It thus seems that from about the middle of the first century A.D. onwards they rid themselves of their monarchical constitution, and were settled down as a political Saṁgha. This is proved beyond all doubt also by a stone inscription found at Bijayagaḍh near Byānā in the Bharatpur State.[2] Unfortunately it is only a fragment of an inscription. But what is

---

[1] CCIM., p. 180 & ff.

[2] CII., III. 252.

preserved is enough to show that it is a record of a personage who was Mahārāja and Mahāsenāpati and also a leader (*puraskṛita*) of the Yaudheya Gaṇa. The title Mahārāja and the word *gaṇa* show that in the year 371 A.D.—the date of the inscription—the Yaudheyas were a *rāja-śabd-opajīvi* Saṁgha. The personage in question was thus one of the Gaṇa-mukhyas. What is worthy of note here is that although he was a Mahārāja, he was Mahāsenāpati. And how could he have been so except on the supposition that before he or his forefather became a Mahārāja, *i.e.* a member of the Gaṇa, he was Senāpati of the royal family of the Yaudheya tribe? The term which denoted 'a general' in the Gupta period is Daṇḍa-nāyaka or Balādhikṛita. The word *senāpati* had long before this time become a hereditary title. This is, therefore, the third instance of a monarchical tribe becoming oligarchic.

Oligarchy was thus one kind of Gaṇa-Saṁgha. Let us see what the other kind was. This kind is represented by the Lichchhavi Gaṇa. I have already told you that it was a federation of the chiefs of the different clans of a tribe who were also each the ruler of a small principality. I have remarked above that it was the custom of a Kshatriya chief backed up by his clan to go on conquering and carving out a small kingdom for himself. It seems that the chiefs of some of the clans comprising the

Lichchhavi tribe had similarly made themselves masters of the different districts and for some time remained independent of one another. A time seems to have come when instincts of self-preservation and safety impelled the various petty rulers to form themselves into a Saṁgha or confederacy. Each confederated principality maintained its separate autonomy in regard to certain matters such *e.g.* as the judicial administration, and allowed the Saṁgha to exercise supreme and independent control in respect of others affecting the kingdom, vesting the executive power in the hands of the select few. I know that perhaps some of you will feel tempted to compare the constitution of the Lichchhavi Saṁgha to the confederation of the German States called the German Empire. I admit that there are some points of resemblance here, but unfortunately we do not know enough about the former to institute any comparison that will be interesting or profitable.

I shall now touch upon two points only connected with Gaṇa. We do not know to what earliest period the existence of this Saṁgha can be traced. Certain it is that they were by no means few in the period we have selected, *i.e.* from 650 to 325 B. C. And they were certainly known as late as the 6th century A.D., because Varāhamihira in his work entitled the Bṛihat-saṁhitā[1] speaks not only of Gaṇarājyas *i.e.*

[1] 4. 24; 14. 14.

kingdoms of the tribal Gaṇas in Southern India but also of Gaṇa-puṅgavas or Heads of Gaṇas such as of the Mālavas, Kaulindas and Śibis. The second point that may be briefly considered is: how did the institution of Gaṇa arise? Did it originate in the political or in the non-political sphere? In this connection let me draw your attention to a passage in the Bṛihad-āraṇyak-opanishad[1]. The passage says that just as Brahman or Supreme Being created the four classes of Brāhmaṇs, Kshatriyas, Vaiśyas and Śūdras among human beings, it created similar classes among the gods also. The Brāhmaṇ amongst gods was Agni, the Kshatriyas amongst them were Indra, Varuṇa, Soma and so on, and Vaiśyas among them, Vasus, Rudras, Ādityas and so forth. And then in connection with the Vaiśya class amongst the gods occurs the following sentence: *sa n=aiva vyabhavat sa viśam=asṛijata yāny=etāni deva-jātāni gaṇaśa=ākhyāyante Vasavo Rudrā etc. etc.* On the term *gaṇaśaḥ* Śaṅkarāchārya comments as follows: *gaṇaśo gaṇaṁ gaṇam=ākhyāyante kathyante । Gaṇa-prāyā hi viśaḥ । prāyeṇa saṁhatā hi vitt-opārjane samarthā n=aikaikaśaḥ.* This gloss leaves no doubt as to the sense in which the word *gaṇa* is to be taken here[2]. And as the passage from the

---

[1] I. 4. 11-3; I am indebted to Mr. R. C. Majumdar for this reference.

[2] I may also mention that Gaṇa (=Vrāta or Śardha) in the sense of a guild appears to have had Vedic precedents as was first pointed out by Roth in the St. Petersburg Dictionary. They are referred to in the *Paṁchaviṁśa-Brāhmaṇa*, VI. 9. 25; xvii. 1. 5. 12, *Vājasaneyi-Saṁhitā*, XVI. 25, and *Taittirīya-Saṁhitā*, 1. 8. 10. 2.

Upanishad speaks of Gaṇas only in the case of Vaiśyas and not of Brāhmaṇs, Kshatriyas or Śūdras, it appears that we had commercial Gaṇas (*i.e.* Śreṇis) first among the Vaiśyas before there were political Gaṇas among the Kshatriyas. If the former is the prototype of the latter, the former must have been divided into Kulas as the latter were. And I was for a long time wondering whether any trace could ever be found of a commercial Gaṇa being divided into Kulas, as no doubt it seemed very natural. I am glad that my efforts have proved successful, and there is now evidence that there were Kulikas even among merchants belonging to a guild. This evidence is furnished by the seals found in the excavations at Bhīṭā and at Basarh[1] or ancient Vesāli, capital of the Lichchhavis. We have here seals not only of

---

1. ASI,-AR., 1903-4. p. 107 & ff; 1911-12, p. 56; 1913-14, p. 138 & ff.; some of these seals have on them the legends: *Śreshṭhi-sārthavāha-kulika-nigama*, *Śreshṭhi-kulika-nigama*, *Śreshṭhi-nigama*, and *Kulika-nigama*. *Nigama* in these legends has been taken to signify a corporation, but there is no authority for it. According to the *Amarakośa nigama* means a *vaṇik-patha*, *pura* or *Veda*. The last sense is of course impossible here. Nor is the first sense practicable, because from Kauṭilya's *Arthaśāstra* (p. 60), we know that a *vaṇik-patha* is a road of traffic whether on land or by river. The meaning is, therefore, unsuitable. The third sense alone is therefore possible, and is by no means unsuitable. This alone can explain why, along with the seals of these Nigamas, we have seals of officials or temples sometimes associated. The seals of officials and temples side by side with those of the Nigamas are intelligible, if Nigama denotes 'a township' but not if it signifies 'a corporation' supposing this sense to be possible, for a commercial corporation is an exclusive body and will not brook the sealing of any foreign member side by side with their own.

Kulikas[1], but also Prathama-Kulikas, meaning Kulikas who apparently were chiefs (of Gaṇas).

We thus see that Gaṇa was one kind of political Saṁgha. Let us now see what the other kinds were. We will here revert to the Greek accounts of the political Saṁghas existing in the Panjāb and Sind in Alexander's time. We have seen (on p. 158) that Curtius and Diodorus mention a people who possessed not one but many cities and whose form of government was not regal but democratic. On the other hand from Arrian we learn that Nysa was a City that was governed by an aristocracy consisting of 300 members and one President. The Greeks were so much accustomed to the nicest distinctions between an aristocracy, oligarchy and democracy that it

---

[Since writing the above, I was able to see the transcripts of the Dāmodarpur copper plates through the courtsey of Mr. Radhagovinda Basak who is editing them for the *Epigraphia Indica*. They belong to the time of the Imperial Gupta Dynasty and are thus contemporaneous with the seals referred to above. While setting forth the administrative details the town officials also are therein specified, *viz.* Nagara-Śreshṭhin, Sārthavāha, Prathama-Kulika and Prathama-Kāyastha. It is thus clear that the word *nigama* of the seals can mean a town only and that in the Gupta period while some towns were administered by Śreshṭhin, Sārthavāha and Kulika together, some were governed by Śreshṭhin and Kulika only conjointly or severally. Along with the Nigama seal was associated that of Kumār-āmātya. This agrees with the administrative fact furnished by the Dāmodarpur plates that immediately above the town officials just mentioned was Kumār-āmātya.]

[1] According to the *Amara-kośa* : *kulakaḥ syāt kula-śreshṭhī*, on which Kshīrasvāmin gives the following gloss : *Kulaṁ kāyati Kulakaḥ, Kulika ity=anye, śreṇy-ādau Śreshṭh-ārthaḥ kule vaṇig-vrinde śreshṭhatvam=asty=asya Kula-śreshṭhī*. Bhānuji Dīkshita's commentary is : *dve kāru-saṁghe mukhyasya*.

is inconceivable that they could have gone wrong in describing these forms of government. When, therefore, we are told that a district containing many cities was administered by a democracy, we are compelled to infer that we have here the government not of a city but of a country, conducted not by a small body but by the assembly of the people. We regret that we are not in possession of more details which certainly would have been very interesting; but what is preserved to us is enough to show that here is the second type of the political Saṁgha that we have to note. But a question here naturally arises: have we got any evidence from the Indian sources which confirms the above reference? I am glad I am in a position to answer this question in the affirmative. We hear of two kinds of popular government: (1) Nigama and (2) Janapada. Both are democracies, but the sway of the first was confined to a single town and of the second extended over a province. Just as we have got the coins of Gaṇas, such as Yaudheyas, Mālavas and so forth, we have coins also of Janapadas which can here denote only 'the people of a country' in contradistinction to the 'tribe' signified by Gaṇa. The latter represents a government by the component families of a tribe and the former, a government of the people, in other words a democracy. Thus we have found one class of coins which bear the legend: *rājaña-janapadasa*=(coin) of the Rājanya people.[1] The word Rājanya here is not a synonym of *Kshatriya* or the Sanskritised form of the Rājpūt title Rāṇā as is commonly supposed but rather the name of a people corresponding to the Rāṇās of the Panjāb hills[2] or Rāṇes of the Goa territory. The second class of coins to be noted in this connection contains the legend: *Majhimikāya Śibi-janapadasa*= (coin) of the Śibi people of the Madhyamikā (country).[3] We thus have at least two instances of Janapada, *viz.* of the Rājanyas and Śibis,

[1] CCIM., pp. 164-5 & 179-80; JRAS., 1907, pp. 92-3.

[2] JRAS., 1908, pp. 540-1. That the word Rājanya denoted a particular people was known even to Pāṇini, who mentions them in his aphorism: *rājanyādibhyo vuñ* (IV. 2. 53). The Sūtra teaches us that if *vuñ* is applied to terms such as Rājanya and others, the word so formed becomes expressive of their country. Thus Rājanyaka means the country of the Rājanyas. Evidently by Rājanya a specific people is meant, a conclusion strengthened by the fact that along with Rājanyas are mentioned Udumbaras, Ārjunāyanas and others who are well-known peoples and who form the *Rājanya-gaṇa* of Pāṇini.

[3] ASIR., VI. 202-4; XIV. 146-7; EHI., p. 213. Madhyamikā is commonly taken to denote Nagarī near Chitorgarh in Rājputānā and identified with that mentioned by Patañjali (IA., VII. 266). But that does not preclude us from taking it also as the name of the province which has the city of Madhyamikā as its capital. We similarly have Avanti and Ayodhyā denoting each both a city and the province of which it is the principal town. In fact, this meaning alone can render the legend of the coins clear and intelligible. That Madhyamikā was the name also of a province is certain. Chapter 32 of the *Sabhā-Parvan* of the Mahābhārata places M(ā)dhyam(i)keyas to the south of Pushkar. Evidently they are the people of the Madhyamikā country, *i.e.* the province round about Nagarī. The *Bṛihat-saṁhitā* also places Mādhyamikas in the Middle Country along with Matsyas. Mādhyamikas here can denote only the people of the Madhyamikā country.

having struck coins. And as issuing coins is taken to be an indication, of political power, this Janapada may rightly be looked upon as a democracy, and hence one distinct form of political Saṁgha. The existence of the Janapada or democratic government in India is traceable to a still earlier period. Thus in the Aitareya-Brāhmaṇa (VIII. 14) we have a passage which refers to the different forms of sovereign power. There we are told that the Rājans of the Prāchyas, the Rājans of the Satvats, and so on, are, when crowned, designated respectively Samrāṭs, Bhojas and so forth, but that the Janapadas called the Uttara-Kurus and Uttara-Madras are styled Virāṭs when they are consecrated to sovereignty. Janapada is here contrasted with Rājan and cited as a form of sovereignty. The natural conclusion is that Janapada is a political form of government which was of a democratic nature and was the rule of a country (as opposed to the rule of a town) by its people. Unfortunately we know nothing about its constitution.

If a Janapada had its Saṁgha or democracy, there is nothing strange in a Nigamà or town having sometimes a similar form of government. Let me here place before you certain facts revealed by works of Hindu Law and epigraphic records. The Vivāda-ratnākara, a treatise on Hindu Law, has a chapter called *Saṁvid-vyatikramaḥ*, in which the various corporate bodies are referred to, and quotes two verses from the Nārada-Smṛiti in which certain organisations are specified, *viz.* the Pāshaṇḍas, Naigamas, Śreṇis, Pūgas, Vrātas and Gaṇas.[1] Now the term Naigama has been rendered by the author of this work as *Paurāḥ*, *i.e.* the body of citizens. We know that the parts into which a country was divided were *pura* or capital-town, *nigama* or mofussil-town, and *grāma* or village. And it is from this *nigama* that the term Naigama has been derived. The law-giver Yājñavalkya[2] too speaks of Naigama as a corporate body along with and distinct from, Śreṇins, Pāshaṇḍis and Gaṇas, and the commentary Bālaṁbhaṭṭi explains the term by *nānā-paura-samūhāḥ*, *i.e.* aggregations of the manifold citizens. But it may be argued that this evidence merely proves that the people of any city could form themselves into a corporation but not necessarily that this was a political body which exercised sovereignty. Now, Sir Alexander Cunningham picked up some coins from the Panjāb and of very nearly the same time as that of Alexander, which, as was first

---

[1] pp. 177 & 180. The word *naigama* cannot mean a guild here, as it has been distinguished from Sreṇin.

[2] II. 192.

shown by Bühler,[1] had all on the obverse the word *negamā* but on the reverse various names such as Dojaka, Tālimata, Atakatakā and so forth. It is natural to take Negamā here to stand for Naigamāḥ, *i.e.* the body of citizens such as that mentioned in the Yājñavalkya and Nārada Smṛitis, and the names Dojaka, Tālimata and Atakatakā for those of the towns to which they belonged. The Naigamas of a town which could strike coinage must be looked upon as a corporate body endowed with political power. This is exactly in keeping with the statement of the Visuddhimagga (Ch. XIV) that some Nigamas or towns and Gāmas or villages also could issue money. In this connection, again, we have to take into consideration the contents of an inscription in Cave No. 18 at Nāsik. The inscription is:

---

[1] *Indian Studies*, III. 49 & n. 1; *Indian Palaeography* (Trans.), 9. Bühler takes *negamā* here to mean a mercantile guild. But the proper word for 'guild' is *Śreṇin* which is so frequently met with in Jātaka literature and epigraphic records. The word *naigamāḥ* again has never been proved to signify a guild. Again, we do not find mention of any guild without the specification of the craft for which it is organised. Besides, we never hear of a mercantile guild having minted any money, at any rate in India. Such a fact would certainly have been mentioned, if it had been really so, in the passage of the *Visuddhi-magga* referred to above especially as the expert knowledge of a *heraññika* or banker is there alluded to and guild coins would have therefore been the first to be mentioned if they had really existed. To say, therefore, that *negamā* of the Panjāb coins stands for a guild is nothing but a gratuitous assumption. It is, therefore, natural to take *negamā* in the sense of *naigamāḥ* (=body of townsmen) such as that mentioned ni the Yājñavalkya and Nārada Smṛitis and distinguished from Śreṇis or guilds.

Nāsikakanaṁ Dhaṁbhika-gāmasa dānaṁ. The natural interpretation is that proposed by Pandit Bhagwānlāl Indraji who says that it records the gift of the village of Dhaṁbhika by the inhabitants of Nāsik.[1] We have here not one individual or a guild, but the whole people of a town, granting a village. And it is inconceivable that they could have done so unless they constituted a government holding sway over the town and its adjunct villages or *nigama-grāmas* as they are called. When we, therefore, find that the people of a city could issue their own coinage and could together give any village in charity, it is difficult to avoid the conclusion that we have here an instance of a Nigama

[1] BG., XVI. 590. This interpretation has been called in question by M. Senart (EI., VIII. 92), who says: "We have met with more than one instance of a genitive joined to the name of a donor, to indicate the community, district or clan to which he happened to belong. I suppose the case is the same here and the Dhambhika village, which had contrived at the common expense (nothing is more frequent than the paying of such religious expenses from the resources of the community) to decorate the entrance of the cave, must have belonged to the general population or to the township of Nāsik." I am afraid, *Nāsikakanaṁ* must mean "of the inhabitants of the Nāsik city" and never "of the clan or district of Nāsik" as is clearly but incorrectly implied by M. Senart (compare *e.g.* Nāsik Inscription No. 22). The suffix *ka* has so far been found applied to the name of a village or town to denote an inhabitant of that village or town. And until an instance is adduced of this suffix being added to the name of a town and of the whole term so formed being used in the plural in the sense of 'district or clan', the interpretation proposed by Pandit Bhagwanlal Indraji seems to be the natural one. Besides, in the Śātavāhana period, not Nāsik but Govardhana was the name of the district.

Saṁgha or town democracy. Nay, towns could sometimes be governed by an aristocracy. We have already seen on the authority of Arrian that the form of government at Nysa was an aristocracy comprising 300 members and headed by the president. This would be another form of Nigama-Saṁgha which is neither an oligarchy nor a democracy.

So much for the different kinds of the political Saṁgha that I have been able to trace at present. There must have been many other types of Collegiate Sovereignty prevalent in Ancient India, which I have no doubt the find of new materials and a re-examination of the old ones will bring to light. A few minutes ago I threw out a hint that the political Saṁgha called Gaṇa was constituted after the model of the commercial Gaṇa. The other political Saṁghas, *viz.* Nigama and Janapada, seem however to be the natural developments of the municipal administrations of towns and districts which were scattered all over ancient India and about which I may be able to say something next year. But the terms Saṁgha and Gaṇa were appropriated also by religious communities, such as *e.g.* Jainism and Buddhism. As regards the Jaina congregation it was split up into Gaṇas, Kulas and Śākhās, a long list of which has been set forth in the *Sthavirāvali* of the Kalpasūtra. And this list not many years ago received a remarkable corroboration from the specification of these Gaṇas, Kulas and Śākhās in the Kushana inscriptions found at Mathurā.[1] The Jaina congregation evidently was modelled after the commercial Gaṇa, or rather after the political Gaṇa, because the founder of Jainism was a Kshatriya, born in a suburb of Vesāli, capital of the Lichchhavi Gaṇa, and himself related to a Chief of this Gaṇa; and it is more natural to think that he framed his congregation after the pattern of the Gaṇa he must have known best. The Buddhist Saṁgha was of an entirely different type. It is true that at the beginning of the *Mahā-parinibbāna-sutta* Buddha advises his Saṁgha to imitate the characteristic concord and amity of the Lichchhavi Gaṇa, but nowhere is it hinted that they were alike in respect of internal constitution. On the contrary, the constituents of a Gaṇa *viz.* Kulas etc. which were the special feature of the Lichchhavi Gaṇa and are clearly noticeable in the Jaina congregation, are, however, conspicuous by their absence in the Buddhist Saṁgha. The latter seems, therefore, to correspond to some Nigama or Janapada-Saṁgha.

It does not require any stretch of imagination to see that these political Saṁghas were of a highly specialised order. We constantly hear

[1] VOJ., I. 169 and ff.

of the councils or *parishads* of the Lichchhavis and their holding frequent meetings. We also hear of *sabhās* and *samitis* of the Nigama and Janapada-Saṁghas. Is it possible to know something about the mode in which they carried on their deliberations? This question must now present itself to us. Fortunately for us the Vinaya-Piṭaka of the Buddhist scriptures has preserved the code of procedure according to which the meetings of the Buddhist congregation were held and conducted. As this congregation was a Saṁgha, it is perfectly intelligible that the set of rules which governed its deliberations must in their essence have governed those of any Saṁgha, be it political, municipal or commercial. Let us therefore try and know from the Vinaya-piṭaka what the procedure of the Buddhist Saṁgha was. You will perhaps be surprised when I tell you that it was of a highly specialised and developed character such as is observed by the political bodies of our twentieth century. The first point to note is the order of precedence according to which seats were assigned to the Bhikshus. There was a special officer whose duty was to see that they received seats in accordance with their dignity and seniority. He was called Āsana-prajñāpaka. We have got a reference to such a functionary in the account of the Council of Vesāli preserved in the Chullavagga of the Vinaya-piṭaka. I quote a passage from it:[1]

"Now at that time a Bhikkhu named Ajita, of ten years' standing, was the reciter of the Pātimokkha to the Saṁgha. Him did the Saṁgha appoint as seat regulator (*āsana-paññāpaka*) to the Thera Bhikkhus."

The deliberations are commenced by the mover who announces to the assembled members what motion he is going to propose. This announcement is called Jñapti. Then comes the second part of the procedure which consists in putting the question to the Saṁgha whether they approve the motion. It may be put once or thrice. In the former case the Karma or ecclesiastical act is called Jñapti-dvitīya, and in the latter, Jñapti-chaturtha. I will give an instance to explain what I mean and shall quote it from the Mahāvagga. Buddha lays down the following rule in regard to the Upasaṁpadā ordination[2]. "Let a learned competent Bhikkhu," says he, "proclaim the following ñatti before the Saṁgha:

"Let the Saṁgha, reverend Sirs, hear me. This person N. N. desires to receive the upasaṁpadā ordination from the venerable N. N. (*i. e.* with the venerable N. N. as his upajjhāya). If the Saṁgha is ready, let the Saṁgha confer

[1] SBE., XX. 408.

[2] Ibid., XIII. 170.

on N. N. the upasampadā ordination with N. N. as upajjhāya. This is the ñatti." Now what follows is Karmàvāchā which is placing the motion before the Saṁgha for discussion and execution (*Karma*), and is in evey case accompanied by the formal repetition of the Jñapti. In the present case the Karmavāchā is repeated thrice. I therefore quote here what follows.

"Let the Saṁgha, reverend Sirs, hear me. This person N. N. desires to receive the upasampadā ordination from the venerable N. N. The Saṁgha confers on N. N. the upasampadā ordination with N. N. as upajjhāya. Let any one of the venerable brethern who is in favour of the upasampadā ordination of N. N. as upajjhāya be silent, and any one who is not in favour of it speak.

"And for the second time I thus speak to you: Let the Saṁgha (&c., as before).

"And for the third time I thus speak to you: Let the Saṁgha, &c.

"N. N. has received the upasampadā ordination from the Saṁgha with N. N. as upajjhāya. The Saṁgha is in favour of it, therefore it is silent. Thus I understand."

As the motion has here been thrice put to the assembly, it is Jñapti-chaturtha Karma, *i.e.* it comprises three Karmavāchās and one Jñapti. A Karma or official act of the Saṁgha to be lawful must consist of one Jñapti and one or three Karmavāchās. When a resolution is placed before an assembly and all the members have observed silence, it is said to be adopted unanimously. If there was any debate and difference of opinion expressed, the matter was settled by what was called *Yebhuyyasikā*, *i.e.* the vote of the majority. This was done by issuing tickets or Śalākās as they were termed. The Bhikshu who collected these tickets was called Salākā-gāhāpaka.[1] If any member of the Saṁgha, owing to illness or other disability, was unable to attend a meeting he was entitled to give an absentee vote which was known as Chhanda.[2] What is more, if at any meeting of the Saṁgha it is anticipated that the minimum number of the members required will not be forthcoming, care was taken to secure the necessary quorum. The 'whip' was called Gaṇa-pūraka.[3] It will be too tedious for me to give a full and exhaustive account of the code of rules that regulated the meetings of the Buddhist Saṁgha, but what I have stated is enough to show you that it was of a highly specialised character. We hear not only of announcing a motion and placing it before a meeting, but also of ballot-voting, votes of absentees, and, above all, the 'whip'—items which we are so much accustomed to think to be characteristic of the modern civilised age that I shall

[1] E.g. *Chullavagga*, IV. 9; SBE., XX. 25.

[2] E.g. *Mahāvagga*, II. 23; SBE. XIII. 277.

[3] E.g. *Mahāvagga*, III. 6, 6 etc. and 26; SBE., XIII. 307 & ff.

not at all wonder if my account appears to be incredible to you. But my authority, the Vinaya-piṭaka, is there before you, and you can at any time read it along with the translation published by Professors Oldenberg and Rhys Davids, and I am sure that you will agree with me in saying that the set of rules for conducting the deliberations of the Buddhist Saṁgha was of a highly developed order, and shows how the regulation of debate was carried almost to a perfection. Again, it is worthy of note that most of the terms technical to Saṁgha debate have nowhere been explained by Buddha. If he had been the first to invent these rules and coin new names for the various procedures, he would have explained them *in extenso*. But nowhere has Buddha told us what Yebhuyyasikā, Chhanda and so forth signify.[1] Evidently he borrows these terms which were already well-known in his time and which called for no explanation. We may therefore not unreasonably conclude that the various terms and rules of debate which Buddha adopted for his religious Saṁgha were those which could fit popular assemblies only and must have already been followed by Saṁghas, whether political, municipal or commercial.

[1] Of course, Jñapti has been fully explained by Buddha, as will be seen from the quotation from the Chullavagga given in the text above. But Buddha is here perhaps singling out one out of many forms of Jñapti prevalent in his time. The details specified by him about valid or invalid Karma, valid or invalid votes, and so on are so many and so complicated that they appear to have come into general cognisance after several centuries' working of the popular assemblies.

Appendix.

I. MANU.

Sānti-Parvan, Chapter 57.

Shaḍ=etān purusho jahyād=bhinnāṁ nāvam=iv=ārṇave
apraktāram=āchāryam=anadhīyānam=va ṛitvijam v. 43.
Arakshitāraṁ rājānaṃ bhāryāṁ ch=āpriya-vādinīm
grāma-kāmaṁ cha gopālaṁ vana-kāmaṁ cha nāpitam v. 44.

[The above verses occur also in Uddyoga-Parvan, 32. 83-4, but without being attributed to any author].

Śānti-Parvan, Chapter 121.

Su-praṇītena daṇḍena priy-āpriya-sam-ātmanā
prajā rakshati yaḥ samyag=dharma eva sa kevalaḥ v. 11.

II. UŚANAS.

Śānti-Parvan, Chapter 56.

Udyamya śastram=āyāntam=api vedānta-gaṁ raṇe
nigṛihṇīyāt sva-dharmeṇa dharm-āpekshī nar-ādhipaḥ v. 29.
Vinaśyamānaṁ dharmaṁ hi yo=bhirakshet sva-dharmavit

na tena dharmahā sa syān=manyus=tan=manyum=ṛichchhati v. 30.

Śānti-Parvan, Chapter 57.

Dvāv=imau grasate bhūmiṁ sarpo bila-śayān=iva
rājānaṁ ch=āviroddhāraṁ brāhmaṇaṁ ch=āpravāsinam v. 3.

[This verse is found also in Uddyoga-Parvan, 32. 57 and Sabhā-Parvan, 55. 14, but without being ascribed to any author].

Śānti-Parvan, Chapter 139.

Ye vairiṇaḥ śraddadhate satye satyetare=pi vā
vadhyante śraddadhānās=tu madhu śushka-tṛiṇair=yathā v. 70.
Na hi vairāṇi śāmyanti kule duḥkha-gatāni cha
ākhyātāraś=cha vidyante kule vai dhriyate pumān v. 71.

Śānti-Parvan, Chapter 57.

Rājānaṁ prathamaṁ vindet=tato bhāryāṁ tato dhanam
rājany=asati loke=smin kuto bhāryā kuto dhanam v. 40.
Tad-rājye rājya-kāmānāṁ n=ānyo dharmaḥ sanātanaḥ
ṛite rakshāṁ tu vispashṭāṁ rakshā lokasya dhāriṇī v. 41.

[These verses have been assigned to Bhārgava. The Bombay and Bengal Recensions have the reading *ākhyāne Rāma-charite nṛipatiṁ prati Bhārata.* This yields no sense, for if *Rāma-charita* is an *ākhyāna* composed by Bhārgava, how can he address any king at all in his own work? Hence I approve of the reading of the Southern Recension, *viz. ākhyāte rāja-charite nṛipatiṁ prati Bhārata.* Here Bhārgava is represented to have recited the verse to a certain prince when he was discoursing on the kingly policy. This sense is perfectly intelligible and natural. Bhārgava must, therefore, here mean Uśanas, originator of a system of Arthaśāstra. And certainly this is not the first instance of Bhārgava being used for Uśanas. In Śānti-Parvan, 210. 20, we have *e.g. Bhārgavo nīti-śāstraṁ tu jagāda jagato hitam*, where Bhārgava who discoursed on the Science of polity can be no other than Uśanas].

III. BṚIHASPATI.

Śānti-Parvan, Chapter 56.

Kshamamāṇaṁ nṛipaṁ nityaṁ nīchaḥ paribhavej=janaḥ
hasti=yantā gajasy=eva śira ev=ārurukshati v. 39.

[This verse is said to have been taken from Bārhaspatya-śāstra].

Śānti-Parvan, Chapter 57.

Guror=apy=avaliptasya kāry-ākāryam=ajānataḥ
utpatha-pratipannasya daṇḍo bhavati śāśvataḥ v. 7.

[Truly speaking this verse has not been ascribed to Bṛihaspati, but is said to have been sung by king Marutta as being approved by Bṛihaspati. What this means is not clear, but it perhaps implies that Marutta was an author belonging to the Bārhaspatya school. The verse occurs in *Ādi-P.*, 142. 52-3 and also in *Śānti-P.*, 140. 48 in the dialogue between Bhāradvāja and king Śatruñjaya which seems to show that the verse is to be ascribed rather to Bhāradvāja].

Śānti-Parvan, Chapter 58.

Utthānen=āmṛitaṁ labdham=utthānen=āsurā hatāḥ
utthānena Mahendreṇa śraishṭhyaṁ prāptam div=īha cha v. 14.

Utthāna-vīraḥ purusho vāg-vīrān=adhitishṭhati
utthāna-vīrān vāg-vīrā ramayanta=upāsate v. 15.

Utthāna-hīno rājā hi buddhimān=api nityaśaḥ
pradharshaṇīyaḥ śatrūṇāṁ bhujaṅga=iva nirvishaḥ v. 16.

Śānti-Parvan, Chapter 68.

Na hi jātv=avamantavyo manushya iti bhūmipaḥ
mahatī devatā hy=eshā nara-rūpeṇa tishṭhati v. 40.

[This verse has been attributed to Bṛihaspati in the dialogue between him and Vasumanas, king of Kosala. That it is an original verse and not a paraphrase or adaptation of it is proved by the fact that it occurs in Manu (VII. 8)].

Śānti-Parvan, Chapter 69.

Kṛitvā sarvāṇi kāryāṇi samyak saṁpālya medinīm
pālayitvā tathā paurān paratra sukham=edhate v. 72.
Kiṁ tasya tapasā rājñaḥ kiṁ cha tasy=ādhvarair=api
supālita-prajo yaḥ syāt sarva-dharma-vid=eva saḥ v. 73.

[The above verses have been assigned to Aṅgiras which is but another name of Bṛihaspati; in the very preceding chapter of this Parvan we find Bṛihaspati styled Aṅgiras (vs. 5 & 61)].

IV. BHĀRADVĀJA.

Manu-smṛiti, VII.

Nityam=udyata-daṇḍaḥ syān=nityaṁ vivṛita paurushaḥ
nityaṁ saṁvṛita-saṁvāryo nityaṁ chhidrānusāry=āreḥ v. 102.

Nityam=udyata-daṇḍasya kṛitsnam=udvijate jagat
tasmāt sarvāṇi bhūtāni daṇḍen=aiva prasādhayet v. 103.
N=āsya=chchhidraṁ paro vidyād=vidyach=chhidraṁ parasya tu
gūhet kūrma iv=aṅgāni rakshed=vivaram=ātmanaḥ v. 105.

[I think, Manusmṛiti has preserved the original verse, and *Ādi-P.* 142. 6-8 and *Śānti-P.* 140. 7-8 and 24 are adaptations of them. Manu VII. 105 occurs with slight changes in Kauṭilīya, p. 29. As the above verses are contained in the dialogue between Bhāradvāja and Śatruñjaya, king of Sauvīra, I have attributed them to the former].

Kauṭilīya, p. 27.

Tasmān=n=āsya pare vidyuḥ karma kiñchich=chikīrshitam
ārabdhāras=tu jānīyur=ārabdhaṁ kṛitam=eva vā.

Kauṭilīya, p. 253.

Kālaś=cha sakṛid=abhyeti yaṁ naraṁ Kālakāṅkshiṇam
durlabhas=sa punas=tasya Kālaḥ Karma chikīrshataḥ.

Kauṭilīya, p. 380.

Indrasya hi sa praṇamati yo balīyaso namati.

V. PARĀŚARA.

Kauṭilīya, p. 13.

Yāvadbhyo guhyam=āchashṭe janebhyaḥ purush-ādhipaḥ
avaśaḥ karmaṇā tena vaśyo bhavati tāvatām.

VI. VIŚALĀKSHA.

Kauṭilīya, p. 27.

Na kiñchid=avamanyeta sarvasya śṛiṇuyān=matam
bālasy=āpy=arthavad=vākyam=upayuñjīta paṇḍitaḥ.

INDEX

[*Abbreviations—Buddh.*=*Buddhist*; *cap.*=*capital*; *cont.*=*contemporary*; *d.*=*daughter*; *dy.*=*dynasty*; *f.*=*father*; *Gk.*=*Greek*; *k.*=*king*; *n.*=*name or note*; *q.*=*queen*; *r.*=*river*; *s.*=*son*; *Sk.*=*Sanskrit*].

C. U. Press—Reg, No. 672—29-5-19—1000.